Whisker Rubs

Whisker Rubs

DEVELOPING THE
MASCULINE ♂ IDENTITY

Don S. Otis

Living Ink Books
An Imprint of AMG Publishers
CHATTANOOGA, TENNESSEE

ISBN 978-089957117-1
First printing—February 2007
Cover designed by ImageWright, Chattanooga, Tennessee
Interior design and typesetting by Reider Publishing Services,
    West Hollywood, California
Edited and Proofread by Kathi Macias, Dan Penwell, Sharon Neal,
    and Rick Steele

Printed in Canada
13 12 11 10 09 08 07 –T– 7 6 5 4 3 2 1

Library of Congress Cataloging-in-Publication Data:
Otis, Don S., 1956–
    Whisker rubs : developing the masculine identity/Don Otis.
        p. cm.
    Summary: "As our postmodern culture seeks to redefine Biblical morality, relationships have taken a serious hit, even within the church. How does this affect men? From boyhood, to the teenage years, and on through mid-life and retirement, the book describes what men in each of these stages of life are dealing with—the challenges they face"—Provided by publisher.
    ISBN 978-0-89957-117-1 (hardback with dust jacket : alk. paper)
    1. Men—Identity. 2. Masculinity. 3. Men—Psychology. 4. Men—Social conditions—21st century. I. Title.
    HQ1090.O87 2007
    305.310973--dc22
                        2006101870

To my three sons: Justin, Curran and Landon.
You belong.
You are valuable.
You are worthy.

Contents

PART II
The Masculine Trip Wire:
Anatomy of Change

PART III
Reclaiming Masculinity:
Beyond the Myth of Invincibility

Acknowledgments

MY FATHER, George Otis, Sr., was a consummate role model. I doubt he set out to be one, but good men rarely do; they simply act on their God-inspired character and instincts. My father did, and I am grateful for his example to me. He was a visionary with drive and determination, a risk-taker, encourager, and lover of people. He held no grudges, saw no obstacles, and made me feel I could achieve great things with divine help. He feared God more than he did failure, and he opened the eyes of the blind to see what could be, rather than what was.

I am thankful to Dan Penwell, Dale Anderson, Trevor Overcash, Rick Steele, and the crew at AMG for believing in this book. And a special thanks to my editor, Kathi Macias, and my proofreader, Sharon Neal.

Countless men have stood beside me, lent their expertise and experience, and unloaded their hearts. Every man needs close male friends, and I am fortunate to have more than one.

Gene Dinsfriend has been like a brother since the fourth grade—nearly forty years. He has listened without complaint, dispensed wisdom, seen my faults, and accepted me anyway.

Jeff Beeman has tolerated my ramblings, shown kindness beyond measure, and joined me on some outdoor adventures I'd rather forget. His selflessness and example are not lost on me.

Allen Wright has taught me that Christian words without actions are meaningless. His investment in me, his mentoring, and his encouragement are what every man needs.

I am grateful to the men with whom I spoke and who gave freely from their own experiences. In mentioning these, I fear I will surely leave someone out: Cec Murphey, the Barnabas of encouragement; my uncle Dr. Duane Walker; Dr. John Carlson; Tim Riter; Dr. Jim Payne; Bob Witte; Rich Middleton; Rafael Barta; Tom Sams; John Hankel; Brian Molitor; Dr. Scott Turansky; Colin Moody; Rev. Eddie Smith; Bob Thorpe; Dr. John Snedden; Rob Henry; Mark Fuller; and Jack MacDonald.

Thanks to my sister and school counselor, Kay Smith, for her wisdom about boys. To Susan Schreer, Sue Nelson, my mother Virginia Otis, and the other women who have given perspective.

Finally, to my three sons: Justin, Curran, and Landon. I did my best to point them to the light and to live in truth. Although as fathers and husbands we are never perfect in our journey, we can and must make adjustments along the road of life.

Introduction
The Birthing Process: Boys to Men

THE YEAR was 1975, after my graduation from four lackluster years in high school. My grades were average, whatever that meant in the suburban Los Angeles school district. I never even took the SAT; it didn't matter at the time. I spent my youth playing sports, doing pranks, or running for my life from an older brother, George, Jr., who had two and a half years on me. By high school, I'd had enough. As many younger brothers who eventually grow up, I took care of business in the only way I knew how—with force. That was the last fight I remember being involved in, but it seemed to settle the matter.

And then it was time for college. I attended for one solitary reason: they had a football team. I was just good enough to play fullback but hopelessly too small at 170 pounds to have a promising career. That was disappointing to me because I loved *doing* football. Being in the presence of other young men is how we males are tested. Our bus rides to Bakersfield or West Los Angeles were never dull. We made the most of the time, exchanging jokes or showing off. The smell of freshly cut grass, ammonia-stained uniforms, sweaty locker rooms, and two-a-day practices in 100-degree heat remain seared in my brain. Even today, the smell of new-mown grass takes me back to the halcyon days of my youth. The naked towel fights, sore muscles, taped ankles, competition, camaraderie, and yes, the pure physicality of the gridiron. The hitting, the running, the coaches with their veins bulging in frustration over a missed block or foiled tackle—it was intoxicating.

I remember one particular fight between two exhausted linemen. It was the end of a smoggy, hot practice session in the middle of summer. The petri dish of masculine angst was ready to explode. And it did. As the two boy-men struggled to express themselves, the head coach did something I will never forget. He stopped the fight and told the two warriors to remove their pads. "If you're going to fight," he said, "do it like men. Do it the right way!" The rest of us, glad for the unplanned respite, watched as the two behemoths swung at each other like drunken sailors. Neither won the fight, and no one cared. It wasn't the point. In fact, I'm not sure there was a point. They were just letting off steam, pent-up frustration, and emotion. This is how boys do it. This is how they have done it since the dawn of time.

Men and brothers have been at each other's throats since the beginning. Cain and Abel's conflict ended with disastrous consequences. Joseph's brothers, out of jealousy, sold Joseph into slavery. David, while a shepherd, had older brothers who chided him for coming to watch the non-battle with the Philistines. Even after David became a king, his sons went at one another. Conflict between brothers and men is to be expected. By trying to eradicate it, we do a disservice to boys by creating weak men. To go a step farther and call it abuse, we stigmatize a process that has been going on for millennia. It's this process that enables boys to try their wings as they learn to fly, and it begins with fathers. There are no shortcuts to this initiation—an initiation that is not only underrated in our culture, but also nearly dead.

Carry on Your Wayward Journey

To this day, I can't tell you why I went. It remains one of the great mysteries of my life. At the end of my first year in college, my dad had "the talk" with me. Bear in mind, I had a job, I had a girlfriend, I was in school, I went to church—what else should a nineteen-year-old be doing? But Dad knew something, the way men know things about other men. Call it a sense, but they just know. My dad knew I was on the verge of floundering, so he stepped in. He could have wrung his hands and said, "I did my best; now it's time for Don to grow up on his own." But he chose involvement instead, and I'm glad he did. Non-involvement would have been easy, but men—if they're real men—don't always take the easy road.

Though I can't recall all the details, the decision was made. I was going to Switzerland to attend *Youth With A Mission*'s school in Lausanne. Why I went, I will never know. Perhaps it was divine providence, a son's obedience to his father, or a sense of adventure. Maybe it was a combination of all three. The bottom line is, I went—and I thoroughly hated it for the first three months. I mean, I *hated* it. My room was little more than a closet; the teaching sessions were painfully long; and to make matters worse, my girlfriend broke up with me. Then, when I was feeling about as low as any man can get, a miracle began to occur. My spoiled middle-class attitude began to crumble. The transformation had finally begun, and I eventually returned home a new person. That experience changed my life, drastically. I went back to college. My run-of-the-mill grades suddenly became As and Bs. My attitude toward others softened. My heart became more pliable. And it happened for one reason— my dad *pushed* me.

In the movie, *Kingdom of Heaven*, the character played by Liam Neeson returns to France after trying to liberate the Holy Land during the first Crusade. There he finds his twentysomething son, a young man born from the older warrior's passion. The son, a blacksmith in a small mountain village, is in mourning for his wife who has just died. The father encourages his son to join him in the struggle to free Jerusalem. At first, the son rejects the invitation, but in time he joins his father and his male warrior friends. As a result, the young man learns about life, about war, about his own identity, about God, and about honor.

Later, as the father is dying from wounds he has suffered in battle, he beckons his son to the church for a special ceremony. With difficulty, the elder stands next to the priest. The son kneels, and the father speaks with conviction to his son. "Be without fear in the face of your enemies. Be brave and upright that God may love thee. Speak the truth always, even if it leads to your death. Safeguard the helpless; do no harm, even if it leads to your death. Do no wrong. That is your oath."

The faltering father removes his ring and hands it to his son. Then he does the unexpected. He slaps his son across the face and says, "That's so you remember it" (the oath). Then he says, "Arise a knight." The moral instruction, the oath, the ceremony—these are lost in modern life, and it's a tragic loss, indeed. The final words of a father to a son speak of honor, commitment, and priority. "Defend the king. If the king is no more, protect the people."

God has placed men in the lives of other men and boys for a purpose—to push them beyond what they think they can do, beyond their zones of comfort. Coaches, dads, brothers, teachers, ministers, and many other men can serve as mentors. Women struggle to fill this role because it's not what God made them to do. No doubt, some will read these comments as the disgruntled ramblings of a misogynist. Let me say from the outset, I believe we have done a disservice to both men *and* women by expecting women to fill roles for which they're neither designed nor prepared. In *Life Without Father,* researcher David Popenoe says, "Fathers have a unique and irreplaceable role to play in child development. Fathers are not merely would-be mothers. The two sexes are different to the core, and *each is necessary*—culturally as well as biologically." Earlier in his book Popenoe writes, "Involved fathers are indispensable for the good of children and society; and our growing national fatherlessness is a disaster in the making."[1] In the following pages, I will examine some of the sociocultural forces contributing to the sense of "lostness" many boys and men feel in our culture.

What Kind of Man Would I Be?

I still wonder what would have happened if my dad hadn't pushed me to leave my comfortable surroundings. What kind of man would I have become? Of course, I will never know. What I do know is this: If my mother had interfered, the outcome would have been different. Suppose she had said, "Don is old enough to make his own decisions. Don't push him so hard." Or, "Why are you being so hard on Don? He's busy with school and doing fine." My mother, God bless her, never did anything of the kind, at least not that I knew about.

There were other, similar lessons for me throughout the years, though most were not as memorable as going to Switzerland to study with YWAM (Youth With A Mission). Nevertheless, even those seemingly insignificant events can be turning points in a boy's life, leaving a positive residue—lessons that we can pass to our own sons. Here's one more personal example to illustrate this point.

Growing up in southern California, I spent copious amounts of time in the Pacific Ocean. Why they named it the Pacific, meaning "peaceful" or "calm," I will never know. As a kid of about six, I recall it was anything but calm when I was sucked to the seafloor by the undertow of a big wave. The washing machine–like movement of the water left me gasping for air and choking on saltwater before I finally stumbled to the shore.

Traumatized, I sat firmly planted on my beach towel for the next four years. No more rough seas for me! Then it happened. We took a family trip to Hawaii, and my dad took it upon himself to "cure me" of my phobia. My brother and dad, heads bobbing on the aqua waters off Kauai, motioned for me to join them. I pretended not to notice, hoping my dad would give up. He didn't. Instead, he came in, grabbed my hand, and took me out past the crashing waves. "See," he said, "it's not so bad out here, is it?" I learned that I could bob on the water, beyond the bone-crushing force of the waves. Then it happened. A rogue wave with its swirling white top was about to crash before it reached the shore. In my bravest voice I said, "Dad, what do we do now?" He grabbed my hand and instructed me to take a deep breath. I did. Under the wave we went—and we survived. After that breakthrough, I spent countless hours bodysurfing Zuma Beach, Malibu, or Santa Monica, zigzagging between waves and enjoying the rides of my life.

Now imagine a different scene. My mom, sitting on the beach next to my sisters and me, sees my dad and brother come in from the water. She tells my dad to leave me alone. She says I shouldn't have to go in the water if I don't want to. After all, she reasons, kids ought to have the freedom to make their own decisions. "Stop badgering the poor boy," she exclaims. "Can't you see that he's afraid?" My dad, effectively dissuaded, capitulates to a higher authority and leaves with his tail between his legs. I have seen this happen many times in other families. If it had happened to me, I would not have enjoyed years of body-surfing adventures.

Most mothers don't understand the dynamic that *needs* to occur between a father and his sons, men and boys, or boys and other boys. There are pivotal moments in a boy's life that mothers cannot afford to dismiss and certainly should not interfere with. Mothers, by nature, are not the risk-takers in the family. They're the guardians of emotion. They're the protectors of feelings, the bandagers of wounds, the information gatherers. A mother, or any other woman, who steps in to meddle in the boy-to-man process, robs a boy of forward progress in his masculine journey. Men push boys. Fathers push their sons. Sons don't always like the pushing, but it doesn't matter. If they can find an ally in their mother, they will, for it's human nature to take the easy road.

Where Do We Go from Here?

This is not a book for the faint of heart. You may not agree with my conclusions, and that's okay. I yearn for the day when men and women can get off Mars and Venus and accept one another for our differences. For that reason I will make the point that gender differences are good; God put them there for a reason. When men and women learn to accept their strengths, weaknesses, and limitations, and stop trying to prove they're gender-tolerant, the social polarity between men and women will begin to crumble. I will also show how society tries to remove the differences, and by so doing, creates further frustration and stress for both sexes. Even with the best intentions, a man can sow bad seed. If he doesn't recognize what he's sowing in his boys, in his family, in their classrooms, in the media—he will reap bad crops. If this sounds like the sordid ideas of a conspiracy theorist or doomsday prophet, read on.

In Part I, "Stages of Bewilderment," I look inside five generational segments—the stages of masculinity. This starts early, goes into the teenage years, early adulthood, middle age, and then the twilight years. In each of these eras, males face something different. Throughout this section, I talked with dozens of men, drew from their collective experiences, and uncovered the kind of struggles, joys, hopes, dreams, and frustrations they encountered.

In Part II, "The Masculine Trip Wire: Anatomy of Change," I examine the reason men feel lost. How did we get to where we are today? What are the influences? Do we even recognize why we feel like we do? "Men's lives have changed too, in ways that are more confusing, more contradictory and often less welcome," says Sean Elder in *Psychology Today*. "Men did not ask to have their lives redefined,"[2] he explains. The sociological survey of current trends gives rise to understanding how the cultural emasculation of men affects the overall psyche of society—almost entirely for bad. Sociologist Andrew Hacker observes in his book *Mismatch*, "Women are now more openly judgmental about men, and with more of a cutting edge, than ever in the past. Epithets like jerk, creep and loser often crop up in accounts of dates that didn't work out."[3] Why is there such antipathy toward men, toward masculinity, or the attributes historically linked to men—leadership, chivalry, danger, strength, or adventure? By trying to level the gender playing field, society has set in motion consequences, most of which cannot be construed as good. In Chapter 9, I look at God's original intent for the sexes. There is a Designer, and by understanding his purpose, men can rebuild on a more stable foundation.

In Part III, "Reclaiming Masculinity: Beyond the Myth of Invincibility," I look at what men must do to reclaim their place in society. This begins by understanding the messages, reorienting our thinking, and embracing who and what we are. This mind-shift is like recalibrating a GPS so the readout is dispensing accurate data. The section examines solutions to the growing chasm between men and women, even within the church.

I argue that most men are positive influences in their homes, at work, and in society. This book is not an indictment of men, any more than it is of women. Rather, it's a road map to lead men back to where we need to be. It's reconfiguring the way we see ourselves. It's reorienting ourselves to the meaning of being a man. It's recapturing, reinvigorating, and renewing our sense of purpose. In other words, it's learning to take our cues about masculinity, about our roles, about relationships, and certainly about fatherhood from those who empower and reinforce, rather than those who tear down and ridicule.

This book is not trying to rally men to a cause; being a man is *not* a cause. Nor is it about stripping women of opportunity or of eliminating their rightfully won positions. My mother is a strong woman. She has a sharp mind and a good sense of humor. Her contribution to my life is no more or less than my father's—it's simply *different*. And it should be. My mother, for all of her self-sacrifice and godly advice through the years, could never replace the role my father played in my life; she isn't supposed to. Likewise, neither could my father step into my mother's role and be anywhere near as effective at nurturing, sharing from the heart, or bandaging hurt egos. I am grateful beyond words for both of them.

Seeking Adventure
A Male Rite of Passage

HE SCENE is set in Montana in the 1850s. The movie is
called *The Cowboys*. A herd of 1,500 cattle has to make it
to market, but the men have left town to chase gold. The
only males in the area are boys and old men. The sixty-year-old
rancher is desperate. What can he do? He walks into the one-
room schoolhouse, sits down in the corner, and observes. The
teacher, a woman, has the children reading from a Montgomery
Ward's catalog. The boys are bored to death. They hate it.
Wouldn't you?

The tall, rugged rancher, played by John Wayne, says,
"Ma'am, if it's okay, I'd like to address these boys before class
breaks up." The teacher responds, "You mean you don't want
to talk to the young ladies too?" "No," says Wayne. "Well, I
guess this really is a man's world," the teacher responds, as she
closes the door behind her. The class full of curious boys wonders what the tough-talking rancher wants with them. Wayne
hires the boys out of desperation. "You're cowboys," he tells
them, "and I'm going to remind you of it every day. The only

way we'll get through is if you obey." Never mind his stern talk; the boys are thrilled.

As the cattle drive is about to begin, one father says to his son, "You have to go out into the world and prove yourself. God bless you, son." The mother is crying. She hugs her son and tells him to be careful. That's what women do; they nurture. Meanwhile, a dozen anxious boys sit atop their horses, waiting for the action. Acres of snorting, restless cattle complete the scene. At last, with the wave of his gloved hand, Wayne gives the order, "Move 'em out!" Smiles erupt on the boys' faces. Finally, they're entering the world of men. Finally, they're going into the unknown. Finally, they're on an adventure.

A boy never becomes a man simply by *going* on an adventure. Rather, the adventure itself *reveals* whether the boy is a man or will ever become one. Believe me; a boy will know whether he's a man after he faces adventure, risk, or challenge. No one needs to tell him; he knows. He might have to repeat the process before he gets it right, but unless he has the adventure, he will never really know, though he will always wonder. He may even find himself in his adult years and realize he must go back to prove himself a man. Most women don't understand this need, but it's there nonetheless. And make no mistake about it; the adventure cannot be contrived, controlled, or predicted. It must be spontaneous. It must test the boy. Most often, the adventure is a physical challenge.

The Nature of the Adventure

The rock seemed like it was fifty feet high, though, of course, it wasn't. It was on the north fork of the King's River in King's Canyon National Park, where our church camped each summer. The giant sequoias, towering granite peaks, and frigid water made me feel alive. The sweet smell of pine, the sound of rushing water, and the fear of bears coalesced in some inexplicable, life-affirming way. In the afternoon, we clambered aboard the bus for the trip to the water hole. That's where the rock was. The anticipation was almost worse than the actual jump. I don't remember the first time I jumped off that rock, nor do I recall how long I stood there before I did. All I remember is that eventually I mustered the courage to leap. Once my feet left the ledge, it was over. As bad as the bone-chilling water felt, the thrill of overcoming the rock was more important.

A boy—any boy—could not stand at the top of the rock for long. There is no hiding what he's up there to do. There is no way to go back down the easy route. He must jump, and he knows it. If he waits too long, he will either be called a sissy (yes, church kids say that), or he will freeze up. That's what happens when a boy or man thinks too long about any adventure. He freezes up. I discovered this truth long ago. The longer that I thought about something I was afraid to do, the harder it was to actually do it. After my near-drowning experience in the ocean, the rock was the next big hurdle that had to be conquered. Every boy has, or ought to have, experiences that push him to his limits. These adventures have certain qualities or characteristics. If you're a dad, or even a single mother, keep these in mind.

1. *An adventure must be exciting.* Take away the element of excitement, and the experience means little.
2. *An adventure must be a challenge.* It must push you to your limit of what you think possible.
3. *An adventure must be unpredictable.* Predictability ruins the serendipitous nature of adventure.
4. *An adventure must tax you mentally, emotionally, or physically—preferably all of these at once.* In other words, it must be hard.

There is a hill by my house. Actually, it's a small mountain over 4,000 feet high, but it's called Gold Hill. The trail to the top is about six miles of twisting, turning, heart-jumping fun—well, at least I find it fun. I ride the trail alone or with my friend Jeff, who happens to have a trip computer on his mountain bike. We hit speeds of thirty-six miles per hour as we descend the single-track trail lined by fir, spruce, and ponderosa pine. One section of the trail is too steep and rocky to ride, at least uphill. We call it the "cutoff" because it links the lower and upper halves of the mountain.

One day Jeff brought Tim to ride with us. Tim is crazy, even fearless, but in a bad way. He has just enough experience to make him dangerous to himself. Men know these things about each other. If you're smart, you don't try to keep up with people like that. The three of us were descending, about ready to hit the steepest section of the cutoff trail, where the only way to ride down is to keep your rear end as far behind the saddle (seat) as possible, and gently alternating between front and rear brakes, let gravity do its job. If you panic and squeeze the front brake too hard, you will suffer the immediate consequences.

This particular day, Tim was riding in front of me. I watched as he hit the front brake and catapulted himself over the handlebars. It was not a pretty sight. He took months to heal. Now, each time I descend that section of the trail, I think of Tim's experience. I feel the adrenaline pumping. I feel my heart rate increase. I feel the excitement. And, thankfully, I sense the need to harness my mental and physical faculties.

The ride up and down Gold Hill fulfills all the elements of an adventure. It makes me feel alive. It taxes me physically. It pushes me to the limits of endurance, strength, and agility. It involves thousands of small adjustments and instantaneous decisions, and it pushes me beyond my level of comfort. That's exactly what boys need, and it's what men need too. We need adventure. We need challenge. As we get older, it becomes self-challenge, meaning we intentionally place ourselves in situations or circumstances that push us to the limit.

Take It to the Limit

Sissy! Wimp! Mama's boy! Nerd! For a boy, these labels sting and sting badly, and they're not easy to forget. For some boys, they lead to a lifetime of trying to prove otherwise. For others, they can easily slide into gender confusion. The messages are clear: different is bad, weak is unacceptable, and soft is feminine. Do these labels make a difference? You bet they do.

In his book *Mentoring Leaders*, Carson Pue tells the story of a man named Dale. Now in his mid-thirties, Dale felt the sting of rejection at age twelve. During a leadership teaching session, the facilitator asked Dale where he saw himself as a twelve-year-old. "I am walking down the hallway of my school and 'the popular girl' of the school, and one whom I really liked, was walking towards me. I was staring at her and she said loudly, 'Who are you looking at GEEK?' "[1] From that moment on, Dale explains, he has been a geek and stuck in some ways as a twelve-year-old boy. Maybe the girl was self-conscious. Maybe Dale was too sensitive. It doesn't matter. What matters is how this man took his cues about himself from a girl before he ever became a teenager.

The playground is the first masculine testing ground. If you measure up, classmates pick you for their team. If you're athletically challenged, you feel the pinch of rejection. No one wants to be an outsider. Each of us wants—no, *needs*—to belong. The pain of not belonging is agonizing. A boy needs to know he fits. If he becomes a loner or an outcast, he can never really shed this label unless he moves to another school, another town, or finds a way to prove to himself that he's got what it takes to be good enough.

Girls don't feel this pressure. Sure, they feel the need to belong, to have acceptance from their peers, to fit in. They want it every bit as much as boys do. What they don't have is the pressure to be courageous, outrageous, physical. They may eventually choose these, but they don't have the pressure early on. Boys do. Richard Land says the adolescent brain is wired for risk taking and novelty seeking. He suggests this opens teens to the vulnerability of consequences associated with experimentation—drugs, sex, reckless driving.[2] Boys are far more prone to this than girls, but it doesn't have to be all bad. I understand Land's point and believe we need to be concerned about mischanneling, but what about positive adventure? A boy who is not inclined to be physical must have a dad or other male figures in his life that push him toward genuine adventure. I use the word *genuine* for a purpose. There are many false adventures. These can take the form of pornography, drugs, sex, or electronic media, but they're not real adventure.

Pornography is a false thrill because it's fictional, and the outcome is predictable. There is no challenge involved. This is why some men choose pornography over real relationships. Real relationships take effort. They require risk. They presuppose the possibility for rejection. Pornography is about quick, easy thrills that never last. It's an adventure with a dead end. Boys need something more. They need something bigger than themselves.

When my youngest son, Landon, was fifteen years old, we took a trip. It wasn't a sightseeing trip; it was a father-son trip, and it pushed the limits. We packed up my Suburban with daypacks, nylon rope, crampons, ice axes, headlamps, helmets, warm clothes, and heavy boots. Our destination: 11,235-foot Mt. Hood, just outside Portland. We arrived late in the afternoon, ate some dinner, looked at the summit in the fading light, and then crawled into our sleeping bags. It was a restive, short night.

The alarm on my Timex Ironman beeped at midnight, signaling it was time to get moving. We pulled on our boots and gloves and adjusted our headlamps. For the first two hours, we stumbled along like a couple of half-coherent drunks. The sky was filled with stars as we made our way over the volcanic rubble. In the distance, we spotted two other climbing parties, their headlamps casting an eerie glow on the glacier above. To the west, nearly two miles below, we could see the lights of Portland. Landon strapped on his crampons, and we roped up for the last thousand feet of the climb. The air was still and cold as the sun began peeking over the horizon to the east.

Gradually, we made our way up the mountain. Neither of us talked. Each step took effort. We just kept moving until I heard Landon mumble, "I'm too tired to go on." I pretended not to hear. We both had a dilemma. What would we do? In the rarified air above 10,000 feet, I had several alternatives. First, I could say, "OK, Landon, you did good. We can turn around now because I understand how tough this is." In other words, I could try to make him feel good for almost making it to the top. My second option was to ridicule him by calling him a "whiner," "wimp," "baby," or any other name that came into my oxygen-deprived mind. Maybe he would feel so humiliated he would keep going. My third option, and the one I chose, was to entice him on—delay a decision and see what happened. We rested. I encouraged him and suggested we climb 200 feet higher to the crevasse separating the rock from the glacier, a tricky part of the climb. He agreed.

We reached the crevasse just as the first climbing party was coming down. The men encouraged Landon, telling him he could make it, that it wasn't much farther. His eyes brightened as these men he'd never met before gave him an emotional boost. I led the brief pitch, then belayed Landon up the ice and on to the last stretch to the summit—400 feet of ice-encrusted rock. Forty minutes later, we stood on the top of Oregon State. We had made it. As far as our eyes could see to the north and south were volcanoes dotting the Cascade Range. But that's not the end of the story.

The descent was easy as we glissaded (slid down the glacier on our coats and used our ice axes as a braking system). Then, Landon said something I will never forget. "Dad, thanks for pushing me. I'm so glad I did it." The tough decision a few hours before turned out to be the right one. As dads, as mentors to other male children, we don't always have a road map. We don't know the way. We stumble in the dark. We hope we're doing the right thing, but we aren't sure. Then, unexpectedly, we receive confirmation.

Boys don't become men in the presence of women. They become men in the presence of other men. They become men when they test themselves. They become men when someone pushes them to the limit of what they think they can do. In a perfect world, dads do this pushing. If a dad isn't around for such a task, or he isn't up to the task, other men must step in.

What Does Adventure Do for a Boy?

I would like to say that adventure turns a boy into a man, but this isn't exactly true. The adventure is a *process* that turns him into a man. Our collection of adventures leads to self-confidence. It makes us believe in ourselves. In other words, all the secular talk about self-esteem is nonsense. How does a boy, or a girl for that matter, develop self-esteem? It comes from accomplishing something big or something important. We do not confer self-esteem on children. We help them *discover* it. We give them opportunity to find it in themselves.

American children think they're smart. For years, well-meaning parents and teachers who want them to feel good about themselves have told them this. But we can't make up for years of child neglect, abandonment, or shoddy parenting by telling kids they're talented when they're not. Who's fooling whom? These kids eventually find out they aren't as good, as smart, or as good-looking as well-meaning adults have said they were. Pushing children, especially boys, to overcome obstacles through adventure builds self-esteem naturally, and they need that to succeed in life. No shortcuts will do. No feminine intervention will suffice. No carefully chosen words will make up for what must happen inside a boy.

When I think of adventure, five principle benefits immediately come to mind. These attributes develop when a boy is pushed toward adventurous living:

- *Adventure builds self-esteem naturally and genuinely.*
- *Adventure builds confidence.* By its very nature, adventure forces boys to be tenacious and to persevere.
- *Adventure develops skills under pressure.* How can a boy learn to make good decisions under pressure unless he's had experience? Adventure hones his skills for quick decision making, thinking under pressure, fatigue, and fear.
- *Adventure builds character.* This is seen on the battlefield where young men are thrust together in a dangerous place. Pressure brings out the true nature of a person. There is no other way to discover this quality.
- *Adventure creates male bonding through shared experience.* Why do men who have fought together in a war form such tight bonds? Camaraderie develops when boys or men spend times of hardship together.

Good Adventure Gone Bad

You cannot eliminate risk and still have adventure. You can minimize risk. You can calculate it. You can plan or prepare for it. In the end, however, you can never completely remove it. The major ingredient in adventure is courage, and this is what boys need. Without an adventure to test their courage, they never really know if they have it. The stories of Huck Finn or Peter Pan show the nature of boys. The countless risks taken by explorers, Pilgrims, or adventurers attest to the sheer abandonment to a goal or set of beliefs. Men are usually on the forefront of discovery, conquering, or keeping the world safe from harm.

Sure, you can argue that men are responsible for war, mayhem, or religious intolerance. Blame it on too much testosterone, sin, ego, insecurity, hate, or bigotry. It doesn't change the truth. Men lead. That's what we do. They die on battlefields, conquer oceans, climb mountains, or do extreme sports. Does this somehow make men better? Of course not; it just is.

In one's quest for adventure, boys and men make mistakes. The risk, no matter how one tries to minimize it, sometimes calls our number—a sheered rope, a chute that doesn't open, friendly fire, a typhoon, a blown tire. You get my point. Is this the time to quit? Let me ask the question another way. Because there is a serious automobile accident on the interstate, do you stop driving? Sure, it may remind you to be more careful, like the white crosses on the side of the highways that mark a past fatal accident. The human tendency in the face of hardship or death is to give up. Many of us do, and sometimes we need to. At other times, hardship is simply part of the equation. There is no perfect formula for every situation. And this is exactly what makes adventure so enticing—the unknown.

A boy has no better teacher than failure. Yet failure implies action, effort, a willingness to risk. A boy can learn more from his failures and insecurities than he can from his victories and certainties. The second triathlon I did was a complete disaster. Halfway into the open-water swim, I started to hyperventilate. People were swimming over me, pushing me under the water. I felt as if I couldn't get enough air. I panicked. I flagged down a small boat, and that was it for the day. It was humiliating, and I was hard on myself. What did I do? Instead of saying, "I just can't swim; this isn't the sport for me," I redoubled my effort. The next month I swam until my shoulders ached, devised a different strategy for open-water swimming (stay on the periphery), and signed up for another race. When race day came, I wish I could tell you I wasn't terrified, but I was. But when I finished the race that day (without drowning), I was thrilled. Since then,

I have done more than a dozen triathlons, though the swim still makes me nervous. For me, failure was motivation.

You *will* fail. Your son will fail. Maybe it's a business deal, a relationship, a race—but whatever it is, life is not over. Your failures do not have to define who you are or what you become. He who fails little risks little. Failure is a sign that you're putting yourself out there. This is not to say that if you're failing at one relationship after another that you should give up. In this case, something else is broken, and I hate to tell you but it's probably you.

There is always balance; men and boys find this balance in the presence of other men—men who are willing to be open and honest with one another. This mentoring process is lost in American culture. We're too independent. We're afraid to reveal our failure, insecurity, or ignorance, so we hide the best we can. In doing so, we hurt our chance for further growth. Boys need to fail; let them. Boys need adventure; give them opportunity. And then watch them grow.

Letting Boys Be Boys
Developing the Masculine Identity

O NE DAY, every boy will face his nemesis. It may be a schoolyard bully, an insensitive boss, an abusive father. There is no getting around it, the confrontation eventually will take place, and the boy had better be ready. If he's not, or if he mishandles it, his identity will be branded—and I don't mean in a good way.

It would be easier, though unrealistic, if life were nice and tidy, but it isn't. Nor is it prudent or realistic to assume a boy can sidestep the process of dealing with life as it comes at him. Only his dad, or other significant males in his life, can prepare him for *his* moment, and a boy must be ready when *his* moment arrives. Sometimes these opportunities come at the most inauspicious times, as author Francis Frangipane so vividly portrays in his book, *This Day We Fight*.

> I was seventeen years old, a senior in high school, and was slouching into my desk when an angry student easily twice

my size . . . burst toward where I was sitting, grabbed me
by my neck and began rearranging my facial features.

I should also mention that at the time I was five feet nine
and weighed 135 pounds. So it was logical that instinct
taught me to "turn the other cheek" in times of conflict. . . .

At that moment, unexpectedly, I discovered another
dimension of my soul: the war mode.

Frankly, I did not even know I had a war mode, but
when the Big Guy reached down to pick me up for "round
two," my fight instincts clicked into action. It had been easy
for him to throw me around when I was not resisting. Now
I sprang upward with a punch that landed squarely on his
nose; he fell back a step. I hit him again two or three times
and jumped on him while he was off balance, knocking him
to the floor. It is possible on reflection that he stumbled
over a chair and my punch had nothing to do with his fall,
but it didn't matter. When his back hit the floor, there was
a 135-pound Sicilian on top of him. . . .

I nearly failed to graduate because of the incident, but
I did not care. Something inside me had grown up and
changed.[1]

Although Frangipane calls this transition moving into the
war mode, it's really about moving into the masculine mode.
There are several elements of his story worth noting. The first is
that many boys are afraid of their test. Although something
inside tells them that one day it will come, many boys do their
best to avoid it. They feel the nagging uneasiness in knowing it
can knock on the door of their masculine self anytime. They can
skirt around the issue or try to avert it by becoming the jokester,
high achiever, or loner, but sooner or later, they need the time to
come—even if they don't win the fight.

A second lesson is that the test, however it may come, is about
discovery for a boy. He learns about his true self. He finds out

whether he has genuine character or just a big mouth. Perhaps more than anything else, this is why boys fear the test. It's a great revealer of who they really are—deep down in their gut. A few manage to sidestep their test indefinitely, choosing the road most easily traveled. If they choose the easy way, they must learn to live with a simmering, self-loathing that can manifest itself through anger or frustration bubbling to the surface at the least provocation. It will then be directed at the weak: subordinates at work, family members, the opposite sex, or even themselves.

A third lesson, and the one that highlights this chapter the most, is what Frangipane says at the end: "Something inside of me had grown up and changed." How did that happen? How does engaging in the battle change a boy, and how does it impact the man?

The Dreaded Test

No great man ever avoids the test. Yes, some dodge it, but they never achieve greatness. Others fail the test miserably, not because they lost the fight but because they ran from it. Consequently, they carry the burden of this failure the rest of their lives, forever trying to prove they're worthy and never believing they are. Others find it to be a welcome turning point in their journey into the world of men.

You will find examples of these tests occurring when a man comes face-to-face with difficult or near impossible circumstances. In the movie, *The Edge*, actors Anthony Hopkins and Alec Baldwin are lost in the rugged Alaskan wilderness. Hopkins improvises, while Baldwin is cynical, conniving, and negative. Hopkins says what is true for all men: "We're all put to the test, but it never comes in the form or at the point we would prefer."

In another movie, *The Gladiator*, a young Commodus arrives on the scene of the battle after it's already over. He asks Caesar, his father, "Have I missed it? Have I missed the battle?" His father replies, "You have missed the war." Many men today are in the same predicament. They have missed the war, and some don't even know it. Others who do know it feel diminished because of it. They don't know what to do, so they grasp at anything that makes them feel in control, powerful, manly. Usually they get it wrong.

God said something to Abraham that might be the most fascinating statement in the Bible. You can read into it anything you like, but it's there. After God asked Abraham to sacrifice his son Isaac, he said, "*Now I know* that you fear God, because you have not withheld from me your son, your only son" (Gen. 22:12, emphasis added). Genesis 22 opens with a sentence containing three key words: "God tested Abraham," and after this fascinating episode, God blessed him. Notice that the blessing followed the successful completion of the test.

As Abraham learned, sometimes one test leads to another and then another. In fact, this is how life works. We don't just face a single test. For boys, however, the test is often a single defining moment—that moment when they must come to grips with who they are. A teenage Jewish boy named Joseph faced his tests too. In historical retrospective, we know the outcome, but at the time, Joseph did not. He had to suffer through uncertainty, interminable patience, frustration, distrust, discomfort, and a host of other not-so-exciting emotions. Any boy, and most men, will deal with similar emotions in their lifetime—including overwhelming uncertainty.

Have you ever wondered why God left Joseph in an Egyptian prison? First, the oversexed wife of one of the most powerful government officials falsely accused him of making sexual advances. Then he was thrown into prison, where he was stuck for years. Joseph might have wondered if all those dreams he had as a kid were the result of bad food. He may have thought, "I tried to do the right thing, and look where it got me!" Maybe you've felt that way before. I sure have. There are times in my life when doing the right thing only landed me in bigger trouble.

It happens that way sometimes. There are no promises from God that making right choices will prosper us, get us a better job, a prettier mate, or kudos from our family. Conversely, sometimes doing the right thing can cost us big-time. That's probably how Joseph felt.

How about David, the boy who killed the giant and lopped off his head with a sword? Do you know what David did immediately after the prophet Samuel anointed him king of Israel? He ran for his life! David's problem was that his father-in-law, Saul, was already the king. For reasons only God knows, he let David know he was "the one" years before the throne actually became his. Apparently, there were tests to conquer and character to be forged. In the meantime, David hid from Saul in caves in the desolate Negev desert. Is it possible David secretly wondered whether the aging Samuel didn't get his message from the Almighty a bit messed up?

Then there is Moses—the prince of Egypt, who ended up spending forty years in southeastern Sinai. Now that is one long test. Perhaps he spent countless star-filled nights trying to figure out why his zeal got him launched into exile. After all, he'd been trying to protect one of his own people, and all of a sudden, he was running for his life. He might have wondered why it seemed that God had abandoned him to this dust-filled purgatory in the desert.

Or Gideon? He was threshing wheat in a winepress, hiding from Midianite raiders. What did the angel of the Lord say to him? "The LORD is with you, mighty warrior" (Judg. 6:12). Gideon must have thought the angel had come to the wrong address. "You've got the wrong man; I'm just trying to survive." Men feel that way at times. Inside they're thinking, "Why me, Lord? Are you sure you don't want somebody more skilled or better equipped?"

Peter had his tests too—denying Christ, falling asleep in the Garden, taking his eyes off the Lord on the Sea of Galilee, getting a rebuke from Jesus. But I don't see Peter as a failure—I see him as a zealous, blue-collar overcomer. Did he learn from his tests? You bet he did. This backwoods country bumpkin and impetuous hothead was transformed into a powerful public speaker who influenced an entire crowd of people—not a bad turnaround (see Acts 2). But remember Peter's personal transformation began with failure.

Your sufferings, your traumas, your disappointments with God or others can be the launching pad to greatness, to learning, and to change. These tests will come and go throughout your lifetime, building or weakening the core of your character. And these tests, whether they come as part of the process of growth into manhood or into spiritual maturity, contain four primary features.

1. *A test that reveals our character.* By successfully passing a test, a man becomes more confident, and thereby his character is strengthened.
2. *A test that often comes unexpectedly.* It can come through a series of events or pressure, but generally the test comes to us.
3. *A test that elicits self-doubt and insecurity and evokes fear.* It brings to the surface the very things we fear most.
4. *A test that most often takes time.* This is not always the case; sometimes it's over quickly. Other times years can pass before the test is over, such as in the lives of Moses, Joseph, or David.

There is no easy way around our tests into manhood, nor is there any easy way to avert them once we become adults. This is not to say the events in our earlier years don't play a significant role in what we become. They do. Sometimes these events make us better. Other times they make things worse or compound our problems. But by far, fathers are the most vital component in preparing a boy to succeed. If you're a single mother reading this book, my advice to you is to ask God to help you find a surrogate father for your son. Mothers cannot raise sons alone, no matter how good a parent they are, no matter how much they love their sons, no matter how much time they devote to the process. In his book, *Iron John*, Robert Bly says, "When women, even women with the best intentions, bring up a boy alone, he may in some way have no male face, or he may have no face at all."[2] As Bly reminds us, only men can initiate boys into manhood.

If you're a father, do your duty. Help your son get ready for the tests he will face in life. If you're a wife, let your husband lead your sons into manhood. You cannot step into your husband's role. If you do, you will hurt your sons, not help them. The most serious consequence of interfering with the tests is how it undermines a marriage. No man wants to engage in a free-for-all with his wife if he has already been through the tests himself. He wants the freedom to help his sons go through their own tests and to schedule opportunities for new tests. Some women insert themselves between the father-son relationships and usurp what God intends, and a son needs to make the transition to manhood.

How the Test Is Won

The wrestling matches in my household were a custom. I'd call it "the rumble." It was a testosterone-filled romp on the floor of our living room. It wasn't planned; it just happened. As the father of three boys, I was seriously outnumbered. In other words, I had to watch my back. The rumble could be playful or intense; it just depended on the circumstances. The sweat dripping from our foreheads or soaking through our shirts reminded us it was purely physical—strength on strength. There were arm-wrestling matches, headlocks, tickling, and plenty of grunting.

Each of my sons developed a different strategy. My eldest, Justin, was the biggest. Eventually I had to give it up, both the arm-wrestling and the wrestling, because he'd annihilate me. My second son, Curran, has a handicap, a muscle weakness in his legs. He was hardest on me—giving me a good head butt on occasion. Next came Landon, who used a hit-and-run tactic. He would wait until I was on the ground with Curran or Justin, and then I would feel his foot in my back or a tug to my hair.

Over the years, I have talked with countless men of all occupations who do the same thing with their sons. I can't tell you where this started, yet it's a vital part of the relationship between young boys and their fathers. I suppose if Jacob could wrestle with an angel, then men can wrestle with their sons. And they do. This is one way for fathers and sons to bond on a masculine level. It's a good way for boys to learn about limits, self-control, and strength. I learned something else whenever we had these rumbles: my wife didn't like them, and she didn't fully understand them. Sometimes she would stay in the kitchen because the entire ordeal drove her nuts. Other times she went into the bedroom to escape.

She didn't get it. Most women don't. If one of the boys got hurt, he ran to his mom for comfort. That's when I knew for sure she didn't like it because she made it a point to let me know about it. But I also remember another pattern. Even after one of my sons left the rumble to seek comfort from Mom, he came back for more. She could never understand how at one moment her son was seeking solace and comfort from her, and the next he was piling on his father's back for more action. The truth is that a boy needs to test his strength, and there is no one better to do this with than his own dad.

When I say the greatest gift a mother can give her son is to let him be a boy, I mean this in the broadest possible terms. She must not interfere with the process. She may not understand it, but she must not interfere with it either. She cannot intervene in her son's fights or his masculine development. She has a different role, one given to her by the Creator—to nurture and love unconditionally. Though she desperately wants to, a mother cannot understand her son's physical tension, and this includes his sexual angst. She cannot understand his drive to be accepted as "one of the guys."

We find preparation for the test in the father-son bond. If a boy lacks a father, it comes from another significant male, like a coach, a youth minister, or an uncle. You can see why fatherless homes place male children at such a disadvantage. To claim, as many in our society try to do, that lesbian couples can raise boys effectively is the height of ignorance. It flies in the face of tradition and conventional studies. Maureen Dowd's book, *Are Men Necessary: When Sexes Collide*, is both patronizing and sexist. It reinforces the mythology that men are superfluous Neanderthals, and that message is not lost on boys. Nor is the message of Peggy Drexler's book, *Raising Boys Without Men*. Because they're asking the wrong questions, their conclusions are false. A more salient question is, "What do boys need for optimal growth into manhood?"

If you're a father, you can help your son prepare for the tests he will face. These are not just my ideas; these are from men who have passed their own tests and come out of the small end of the funnel with strong character.

1. *Step up to the plate.* Be willing to take a risk. Those most likely to succeed at their tests are willing to risk striking out. This means being in the right place when the test finally finds you.
2. *Be patient.* Your job is to prepare your son to pass his test when it comes. Sure, you can stage mini-tests to see how he will respond in uncomfortable or challenging situations, but ultimately he will have to find strength within himself.
3. *Do what you know is right.* As Joseph did, do the right thing because it's right. Boys need to know that doing what's right can be costly. As fathers, we must not whitewash this possibility. While we may desperately want our sons to develop integrity, they must discover it through the choices they make.

4. *Don't be passive.* Passivity is not what a boy needs when he's faced with a giant. He needs courage. He needs boldness. He needs a quick decision. These qualities must be near at hand when he needs them most—at the time of crisis.

5. *Harness your fears.* Fear is normal. Teach your son to get used to it. The test is always accompanied by fear. Those who are accustomed to fleeing when the heat gets turned up will wither under the pressure. Teach your son to stand his ground, regardless of how he feels. We live in a culture where feeling predominates. This makes for weak men and feeble boys.

6. *Listen to wise men.* Boys learn masculinity in the presence of other men. If you're a father, speak into the life of other boys, and encourage your trusted male friends to speak into the life of your sons. Encourage your sons to participate in sports, scouting, or other activities where boys spend time with boys and other men.

7. *Don't fear failure.* Failure is a stepping-stone to success. It's a natural inclination for boys to let failure define who they are. Had Peter done this, he would have been worthless on Pentecost. Instead, encourage tenacity, perseverance, and grit. It's easy to quit. It's harder to keep going when all seems lost, when we're losing the race.

Winning Isn't Everything, but It's a Lot

I was in fifth grade, and Chris was a grade ahead of me. He was tough, a good athlete, and he wanted to fight. To this day, I have no idea what I did to provoke the fight. Probably nothing. All I remember is that I was scared. I knew I couldn't back out; there was too much at stake. Word about the fight spread throughout our suburban Los Angeles school like wildfire. For the rest of the day, I could think of nothing but the impending fight.

After school, it seemed the entire student body of Kittridge Elementary was walking to the vacant lot a half mile away. It was showdown at OK Corral, and I knew I would lose. Even with this knowledge, I still had to do it. There was no backing out. As dozens of kids gathered at the lot, Chris and I went at each other. It wasn't a pretty fight. Neither of us really knew how to do it right. A left to my face and blood started trickling down the corner of my mouth. I landed a couple of feeble hits that sent him stumbling backward into the dirt. A mix of sweat, blood, testosterone, and dirt filled the dust-choked air. Our clothes were ripped, our hair matted. Before we knew it, the fight was over, thanks to a kindly neighbor who came over to break it up. I was grateful that he did, and I think Chris was too.

I don't know if either of us "won" the fight that day. It didn't matter. What I do remember is that Chris and I became friends after that. Something inexplicable happens when boys or men face their tests. They develop a respect, a bond. They know they have been through the fire and come out with their reputation intact. Crisis, even the self-imposed kind, bonds boys and men in ways little else can.

I'm not going to say that winning isn't important; it clearly is. What I am saying is that often it isn't about whether you win or lose; it's whether you show up for the fight. It's far worse not to show up for the fight than to show up and lose. Most boys know this intuitively. If the fight is analogous to the test, and I believe it is, then showing up is half the battle. This is not to suggest it's advisable for boys to prowl for fights so they can test their manhood, though some do. This isn't what true masculinity is about. It's about rising to the occasion when a clash is necessary. This is where men and fathers offer help—mainly by understanding the nature of the battle. Not by helping their sons avoid the test, but by helping them conquer it, for that's what men do.

Let It Be: A Boy's Struggle
against Feminine Identification

Let's face it, mothers lessen pain. They bandage wounds and bestow comfort. They're the soothers of bruises, not the initiators into bruising. Author Steven Bly explains the blows a boy receives from his mother:

> "You're frail, you know; you shouldn't play with those boys."
> "How could you kill such a beautiful little bird?"
> "If you don't stop that I'll send you to a foster home! See how you like that!"
> "You're too big for your britches."
> "Now you're acting like your father."[3]

These blows are often inadvertent, barely recognizable by the mother if recognized at all, and they're spoken out of exasperation, desperation, exhaustion, naiveté, or hurt. They often come from the nurturing, protective, feminine side, though of course, not all mothers are like this. But for the most part, a mother's job is to make the hurt feel better, to protect her son from harm, to make the pain go away, and to receive love from him. The father, however, realizes there is a purpose in his son's pain. He knows this because he too felt, or still feels, pain from his own wounds. He wants his son to embrace his hurt, to pass his tests, to overcome hardship—not through avoidance, but through acceptance of the pain. It's through the pain, hurt, challenge, or tests of life that a boy grows in character. There is an integral link between his strength and his self-esteem. He must navigate the tender ground between running toward the feminine and embracing the masculine. He needs and wants both, but with the help of his father, he gradually weans himself from his mother and begins to look for direction from men or peers.

Some wise women understand their son's need for emancipation. They don't like it, but they know it. The boy must leave the dependence of the breast that nursed him. He must move out into the unknown seas, into adventure, risk, rejection, hurt, and yes, even into pain. His mother cannot follow him there; she can only watch from afar. She can offer solace when the boy-man feels pain, but she must let it be *his* pain. Sensitive fathers understand the emotional tornado that wreaks havoc in a mother's heart, and his tenderness can shorten her time of grieving.

If there is tension between a mother and father, a boy knows this. Some mothers will exploit this strain through emotional enmeshment with their sons. This delays or destroys a son's journey into manhood. It also exacerbates the rift between the husband and wife, leading to separation or emotional distancing. A mother who sees her sons moving away from her can do one of two things. She can recognize the shift as the son's attempt to move into the world of men, the world of responsibility and maturity, or she can hold on tighter reasoning that her son is not ready yet, and when he is, she will set him free. But she rarely does. She clings to him, and she does so out of her own need. These mothers see the boy-to-man process as a boy's rejection. She feels the impending loss and internalizes it. She may even blame the father for turning the boy against her. And believe me, a boy feels this pressure. He's caught between countervailing forces. He doesn't want to displease his mother, but he knows his own need to become a man. If a woman takes this route— injecting shame or guilt-pressure on her son—it will create one of two negative outcomes that I will explain in a moment.

It's difficult enough for a son to leave safety and comfort for the unknown. There are many men in our culture who do not know how, or simply refuse, to be men. Somewhere in their development they failed. They ran from the tests, had a father who was emotionally or physically absent, or a mother who held on too hard. A man whose self-esteem is weakened, for whatever reason, will flounder. He will act like a fish out of water, exerting great amounts of energy but remaining stuck in a world that is not his own. He's vulnerable to an enemy he doesn't understand. This is why male initiation rites are so vital. America has lost these rites, if we ever had them. Typically, initiation ceremonies occur in societies that emphasize the importance of the extended family unit. Since this traditional structure is in disrepair or undergoing sociological devolution in Western culture, boys are left to figure it out on their own.

The first of several negative outcomes when boys are deprived of this necessary rite is that they grow up weak. They rarely achieve their full potential. Inside they know they could have been more, but they don't know that it's primarily the fear of failure, of not measuring up, that holds them back. A second negative outcome is that many of these boys, particularly the strong ones, develop resentment for their mothers. It becomes a breaking away from their mother on their own terms. This kind of transition is always harder for the mother *and* for the son. The weak ones remain emotionally wedged in their mother's womb, trapped in the comfort zone. They're frustrated, lost, and wonder why life is passing them by.

A fifty-year-old friend told me about his own resentment for his mother. His dad, a traveling salesman, was frequently on the road. When his dad was away, his mother had him sleep in her bed. Although nothing inappropriate ever happened, an eleven-year-old boy knows he has no business in his mother's bed. He said, "This is one of those maternal-imposed wounds I'm not happy about and would prefer to keep repressed for the sake of peaceful relationship in her twilight years."

The mother, to meet her own needs, uses the son, as my friend's mother did. If the boy feels used, he grows up with a jaded view of women. He may begin to mistreat his mother for putting him in such a place—an unconscious way of distancing himself from her and breaking free of her influence. In some instances, the boy may grow up with an unbalanced view of women. His subconscious shame may lead him to see women as untrustworthy. He believes they're trying to rob him of his masculinity. His romantic relationships suffer also. He may find it hard to get along with female employees or bosses. This is not to say he isn't responsible for his choices; it means his perception of women is branded by the maternal wound. If his future relationship with women is to be healthy, he must recognize his wound, learn to trust, and forgive his mother.

One mother of a teenage boy was afraid to let him drive. Each time she rode in the car with him, she would correct him or express fear. He got the message. For a boy, here's what that mother's verbal and nonverbal behavior says: "You're not ready," "You're not good enough," "You don't measure up." And this is the message many men feel in relationships with their women. They carry their wound of rejection, internalize it, and carry it as if it were a Sisyphean duty—which it isn't. What did this mother fear? Did she consider the larger implications to her son's psyche? No doubt she felt she was "protecting him." If this is what mothers do when boys are young (and they should), they need to take a different tack when their sons get older. A mother's comments can create a self-fulfilling prophecy for a son. He thinks, "If she doesn't think I can do it, maybe I have no business trying." He trusts her, implicitly, and so he gives up. He stops trying to enter the bigger world, a world fraught with risk, mistakes, and pain. Inside something dies. If his father or another male figure doesn't intervene, the boy will falter. If the mother, whether consciously or unconsciously, seeks to protect her son from the father, she risks bitterness from both. More importantly, she places her primary relationship—her marriage—in jeopardy.

The boy, or man, learns something else: The woman, the mother, the wife must be disappointed in him. He thinks, "I must not be good enough, or she would be happy with me." Many men feel that nothing they do is ever quite good enough. The boy or man who feels this way initially embraces the fantasy that if he tries a little harder, maybe she will accept him, but he soon discovers this tack doesn't work. What most men don't know is this: She isn't just unhappy with him; she is unhappy with herself. A boy caught in this vicious trap is forever trying to prove he's good enough to the woman—any woman. It's as if he's crying out for acceptance, recognition, and respect. At its worst, he grovels for feminine attention or sees the woman as a conquest. If he chooses the latter, he often engages in multiple sexual experiences—conquering and pleasing women but giving them little else. This is not how God created men and women to relate. And this is one reason women feel used by some men, and why some men struggle with intimacy (fully giving themselves to their woman).

P A R T

I

Stages of
Bewilderment

Little Boy, Be Good
Social Pressures to Tame Boys

NOTHING IS so exhilarating in life as to be shot at without result," quipped Winston Churchill. He was audacious, wasn't he? Yet by the time he was forty years old, Churchill said, "I am finished." That was 1914, long before Hitler came to power in Germany. Though the great English statesman suffered bouts of depression, loss, and disappointment, Churchill always managed somehow to bounce back. He obviously practiced what he preached when he said, "Success is the ability to go from one failure to another with no loss of enthusiasm."

Like other great men Churchill failed many times, but his keen sense of humor carried him through many down days. He was quite intelligent, though few people know that he had been a very poor student, consistently at the bottom of his class. Many years later, he told a Harvard graduating class, "The empires of the future are the empires of the mind." Empires of the mind? What an interesting quote from this statesman, prime minister, soldier, orator, painter, and writer. Churchill could have let his feeble academic record define who he became, but he chose not to. He persevered because that's what mature men do.

Churchill discovered a love for books, for history, for English, for adventure. He coined the term—*live dangerously*. Yes, it was Churchill—not Nike or the Xterra marketers. He was fearless, willing to try anything. Like great men before him, he shared a passion for action and adventure.

Now let's imagine another Churchill. His teachers tell him that unless he gets serious about his studies, he will never amount to anything. He's told to settle down and behave, to stop fidgeting, doing pranks, or daydreaming. Yes, boys do these things, even in the best of schools. I know because, like other boys, I was always dreaming about recess, the next prank, or the cute girl across the classroom. To me, except for the social part, school was akin to torture. And from kindergarten to seventh grade, I never had one male teacher.

A Gender-Based Caste System

My boys still remember it: "The Wall," where Ms. Taylor stood watch like a Nazi sentry, looking for the slightest infraction on the play yard. Her voice would rise a few decibels when a boy—any boy—caught her eagle-like gaze. Boys! That's what Ms. Taylor was after. Like a huntress waiting for her prey, her scowl could melt a sensitive boy. She showed favor to girls, while holding boys to the harshest of standards. And it wasn't right. In hindsight, she had no business working in a school, but there she was. Ask any boy, or now a few men, and they will tell you the same thing: "Ms. Taylor was a b——." Yes, a harsh word, but that's what comes readily to their minds.

The Wall was Ms. Taylor's way of meting out punishment. My sons don't remember a girl standing against the wall, ever. It was always boys—the troublemakers. They were too active, too disobedient, too whatever.

I am not an advocate for ignoring serious disobedience. Yes, sometimes "boys will be boys," but this doesn't mean we should tolerate rebellion. Nonetheless, some women:

1. Punish boys for the insensitive way certain men in their lives have treated them.
2. See the energetic behavior in boys as bad (or rebellious).
3. Recognize the differences between boys' and girls' behavior and accept these as part of God's design.

In these examples, boys hear the following message: "Slow down, settle down, be nice, and be calm." They get another message too: "Don't make a woman angry." While some boys ignore the subtle messages, sensitive ones do not. The sensitive boys believe they must appease the woman, any woman, and soon find themselves trying to do just that. These boys have an intuitive sense that they must tiptoe around many of the women in their lives. They fear they will arouse her ire or face interminable questioning (whether true or not, men interpret this as control). Ever wonder why so many women say things like, "He just won't talk to me"? There is a reason. And the reason rarely has anything to do with a man's capacity to listen. Rather, it has more to do with his fear that by opening up he's making himself vulnerable to her verdict about him. Most men won't go there because they don't feel safe, and this pattern starts very early in life.

Clever or deceitful boys may grow up to sidestep, circumvent, or try to control the women in their lives. But they don't fully give themselves to them. Good women don't understand this behavior in men, precisely because they don't understand the messages boys grow up believing about women. They scratch their heads and say, "I just don't understand men." And many women don't. The experiences of young girls growing up are quite different from boys. In grade school, girls are part of the Brahmin caste, and privilege rarely sees itself as such.

There is something else. Boys, or men, for that matter, who don't behave themselves often find the twin towers of guilt and shame bearing down on them. Yes, some women use these tools subconsciously, believing that the men in their lives will come under their spell—or control. Men who succumb to shame become weak men. They're often indecisive in life and vocation. They frequently seek out the approval of women, yet they fear they will be judged by them and come up short. As John Eldredge puts it in *Wild at Heart*, "No matter how good a man you are you can never be enough."[1] He went on to say that deep down in the guts of most men, there is a fear that what we have to offer a woman won't be good enough.

The sense of not measuring up begins most earnestly in the elementary years, but not in the home. In the home, a boy is under the emotional protection of his mother, or should be. For good or ill, the formative elementary years leave an indelible impression on young boys about the opposite sex. Once he becomes a man or at least looks like one, he may find it difficult, if not impossible, to measure up in his significant female relationships, particularly with his girlfriend or wife. If he takes his cues about who he is as a man only from female teachers, bosses, his mother, wife, or sisters, he will become a weak man.

Never Quite Good Enough

A strange phenomenon occurs when scrambling over granite slabs to find the top of a high mountain peak: You discover false summits. You're tired and exhausted, looking for something to encourage you on your journey. Then you see it, the top of the mountain—or so you think. Instead, it may be one of many false summits. No matter how much you wish you were there, you know it's just another cruel trick, like Sisyphus rolling the boulder up the mountain only to see it tumble down again. Men often feel this way: "Can I ever be good enough? No matter how hard

I try or what I do, will I ever be good enough?" Even when a man does the right thing, he often senses the critical eye of judgment upon him. If he's a sensitive man, this feeling of rejection can overwhelm him. And many men today feel overwhelmed. What's he supposed to do? How's he supposed to behave?

David's response to his wife Michal (Saul's daughter) provides an answer. Obviously, King David understood that men find their sense of self from God—not from Eve. He experienced the kind of shaming and disappointment I'm talking about when he returned to Jerusalem with the Ark of the Covenant, dancing and praising God in front of all the people. His wife was none too pleased with his theatrical performance.

"David, wearing a linen ephod [an outer vestment worn by priests], danced before the LORD with all of his might . . . As the ark of the LORD was entering the City of David, Michal daughter of Saul watched from a window. And when she saw King David leaping and dancing before the LORD, she despised him in her heart" (2 Sam. 6:14, 16). Michal could not keep her displeasure to herself. When David came in to bless his family, he ran head-on into one disgruntled woman, who said, "How the king of Israel has distinguished himself today, disrobing in the sight of the slave girls of his servants as any vulgar fellow would!" (v. 20).

Ouch! Here was the king of Israel, returning from a joyous event—call it a victory, if you want—and his wife immediately judged him. David was not the first, and he certainly won't be the last man to feel his wife's wrath. Here's what Michal's response tells us.

1. She *despised* him (another word for hate).
2. She was an *observer*, not a participant, in honoring the Lord.
3. She used *sarcasm,* a form of guilt and shame, to ridicule her husband.
4. She *judged* his motives falsely.
5. She came under God's *judgment* (she was barren her entire life).

David, to his credit, handled the criticism well by saying, among other things, "It was before the LORD." He reminded her of who he was—God's chosen man. He told her, "I will celebrate before the LORD. I will become even more undignified than this, and I will be humiliated in my own eyes" (vv. 21, 22). Now that is the kind of response a man gives!

I wonder how I would have handled the same situation. How about you? If David took his cues about leadership, about spirituality, or about his behavior from the woman in his life, he would have been a miserable failure. And it would have been easy for him to do so. If he were insecure or overly sensitive (as many men are today), he might have said, "Did I look that bad in front of the people?" "Do you think they lost respect for me?" "I am so sorry for embarrassing you." In so doing, she might have been appeased . . . for the moment.

Don't we tell men to be sensitive to their wives in public? David wasn't. Don't we tell men to listen to their wives? David didn't. David blessed his family, honored the Lord, and showed his emotions in public. For these acts of righteousness, the primary woman in his life ridiculed him. Maybe this has never happened to you. If so, consider yourself fortunate. Maybe you see this as an isolated story. Believe me, it's not. For many men, Michal's response resonates like a punch to the solar plexus. Men feel the pain. They sense the tension. Like running headlong into Ms. Taylor's Wall, they feel that no matter what they do, it won't quite please her. Some men stop trying altogether. Others find another woman to please. Still others, like David, recognize appeasement as a dead-end street.

Twenty-first century men may not face the same kind of challenges as men in 1000 BC. Nonetheless, the relationship between men and women has changed little since Adam and Eve and the Fall. Today, the mitigation of this underlying tension comes in diverse and often contradictory forms—kindness, mutual respect, pacification, and role reversal, just to name a few. In education, however, the Wall is becoming a perfect metaphor for how boys feel the sting of marginalization.

The Education Conundrum

I know facts are tedious, but sometimes they help emphasize a point, so please bear with me for a moment. Girls are now out-performing boys from kindergarten to graduate school. More girls receive bachelor's degrees (young women receive 133 for every 100 that young men receive). More boys are in special education classes (70 percent). They have a higher drop-out rate (30 percent higher than girls). Ninety percent of the Ritalin users (to combat Attention Deficit Disorder) in school are boys.[2]

Girls read more books. Boys are more involved in drugs, alcohol, and crime, and they commit suicide at a greater rate. And it gets worse.

A mere 21 percent of the nation's teachers are men, the lowest ratio since the mid-1960s. Not unlike my own grade-school experience, just 9 percent of elementary teachers are male.[3]

About 300,000 more women than men enter graduate school every year. According to Dr. Michael Thompson, the author of *Raising Cain*, "Girls outperform boys in elementary school, middle school, high school, and college and graduate school." In other words, boys are falling behind, and fast. As Thompson notes, "Girls are soaring while boys are stagnating."

These trends raise three salient questions:

- How did education get so lopsided?
- What are the long-term consequences?
- What should be done?

To answer the second question first, the economic engine that keeps America strong could fall into serious trouble. If current trends continue, the last bachelor's degree to be earned by a male will occur sixty years from now; from then on, all recipients will be female. The imbalance has little to do with mental acuity and almost everything to do with methodology. As men take on more blue-collar professions, women will move rapidly into professional positions, including leadership posts. I'm not making a value judgment about women in leadership, and in many instances, they do a much better job than most men do. I am expressing, however, serious concern about how this reads out in our male population.

Paradoxically, boys have a far greater academic range than girls. And, according to Thompson, while there are statistically more boy geniuses than girl geniuses, far more boys than girls are found at the very bottom of academic ranks.[4] Whether the range is due to design, socialization, teaching, or some other variable doesn't really matter. What matters is that there is a difference.

There is no single answer to the first question of how education has become lopsided. There is, however, plenty of conjecture. Four major influences stand out in my mind, which I've listed and then I'll make brief comments about each.

1. Feminism's effort to level the academic playing field at any cost
2. Fatherlessness and the lostness of boys
3. Ineffective teaching methodology (for boys)
4. Unwillingness to recognize gender differences in learning

According to author Christina Hoff Sommers, in order to advance girls, the feminist movement exaggerated how vulnerable girls were, while at the same time understating the needs of boys. They depicted boys as the privileged beneficiaries of a flawed patriarchal system that opposes women. Sommers believes women teachers favor girls over boys because their classroom behavior is often more conducive to traditional learning.[5] Boys notice this and quickly realize the environment is not male-friendly. Some then opt out of a process they believe is stacked against them.

Secondly, if the cards are stacked against boys in school, they're also stacked against them at home. Boys who come out of fatherless homes don't do as well in school, have higher rates of criminal behavior, commit suicide more often, and drop out at higher rates than boys from homes with dads. If boys are already struggling with rejection from a biological father, imagine what it's like for them to submit to similar rejection in school. Even boys from intact homes have an uphill battle. Some boys—and many men—will give up on a relationship, on a job, or on school if they feel they can't win. If you wonder why there are so many so-called deadbeat dads, perhaps you should look at what's really going on inside the minds and hearts of these men. Undoubtedly, some are selfish, narcissistic, lazy, or lack commitment. Yet there are others who have been driven out of their homes by lack of respect, marginalization, or pervasive ideologies that make them want to flee. Regardless of the reasons, boys and girls suffer when men leave.

Thirdly, the learning process is geared toward girls. This is no surprise. As Sommers notes, "If boys are obstreperous and high-spirited and competitive, which most of them are, this is seen as behavior which is not tolerated. They [educators] see this as an expression of toxic masculinity."[6] Speaking from personal experience, most boys don't do particularly well when they have to sit all day. Did you ever look around church to see how many men are not there? Is this because men are less spiritual? I don't think so. Rather, the lecture-hall setting just doesn't do much for men. "If you listen to 10- or 11-year-old boys, you will hear that school is not a very happy place for them," according to Bret Burkholder, a counselor at Pierce College in Washington State, who also works with younger boys as a baseball coach. "It's a place where they're consistently made to feel stupid, where girls walk around in T-shirts that say 'Girls rule, boys drool,' but if a boy makes a negative comment about girls he'll have the book thrown at him."[7]

Fourthly, since elementary teachers are predominately female and classrooms typically run the way they have for one hundred years, chances are good the public system will not change anytime soon. Imagine if someone proposed segregating girls and boys. Or suppose someone suggested boys be taught in a different manner than girls (which needs to happen). Actually, someone has. During an interview on National Public Radio's *All Things Considered*, boy's author Jon Sciezka said, "[Society is] promoting such a narrow version of literacy that we're not including what a lot of boys like." Of course, Sciezka's approach is to include humor and silly stories that resonate with boys. But regardless of whether or not we agree with his proposed solution, his premise rings true—treating boys and girls the same in school just doesn't work.

This conundrum begins early, even imperceptibly, and gains momentum as a boy runs the gauntlet of public education.[8]

Snakes and Snails

If girls are made of sugar and spice and everything nice, why are boys made from snakes and snails and puppy dog tails? I know it's a cute rhyme, but the point is clear—and not so cute. Boys are not nice. Girls are. Boys are troublesome, overactive, and rascally. Girls are compliant and sweet. Guess what? Schools take this to an illogical extreme, with one of the results being that boys are overmedicated to calm them down. As noted earlier, the vast majority of children on Ritalin are boys.

Boys who are bored, but active, often receive the label of "learning disabled." They see themselves as "stupid" and begin to tune out at school, compounding the problem for educators and students alike. This vicious cycle comes from our social penchant to pathologize virtually every apparently aberrant behavior. Three-quarters of children labeled as learning disabled are boys. What does a label like that do to a sensitive boy?

Instead of channeling boys' natural aggressiveness into positive arenas, the nature is ignored, suppressed, and wished away. What is so dangerous about the feminized worldview of male nature is that when treated with respect and discipline, boys can learn appropriate behavior and mature into normal healthy men. It's not surprising, then, that tales of restlessness and of boisterous boys disturbing classrooms or recess have been mounting for years. More and more boys are put on Ritalin or other drugs to correct their behavior, with little or no distinction made by experts between real misbehavior and boyish rambunctiousness.[9]

Some experts, like Dr. James Dobson, believe schools do not intentionally single out boys. Instead, the way boys are treated is the way schools have always functioned. The problem is endemic; it's institutionalized. This makes correcting the problem even more difficult, like trying to correct false theology within a denomination. In his book, *Bringing Up Boys*, Dobson says, "I've met thousands of little immature troublemakers through the years who drove teachers crazy. In fact, I used to be one of them." He goes on to say, "They [boys] are in agony when required to endure long periods of relative inactivity, a prohibition on noise, and an environment where everything is nailed down tight."[10] Dobson is right. He understands the testosterone-induced frustration resulting from such classroom settings, which many boys endure like a trip to the dentist.

Finding Balance: Letting Boys Be Boys

Mrs. Bergino was a nice woman and a good teacher, but she just didn't "get" boys. In the fourth grade, recess and lunch is everything to a boy—at least, it was for me. For Mrs. Bergino, recess meant jumping rope, something I hated. The other boys hated it too. But the girls were amazing. They could jump two ropes at a time, while the boys looked on in starry-eyed wonder. We asked ourselves, "How can they do that?" We wanted to run and holler, not stand around watching girls jump.

The boys begged and pleaded every day, every week, all year long. At times, it seemed we were up against an immovable force. On a rare day, we got the bats and balls out and hit the rubber softball as hard as we could. That's what we wanted to do—hit the ball and run the bases. As I look back on it now, if Mrs. Bergino, or any other teacher, had told the boys to run the perimeter of the schoolyard, we would have been calmer during class, and much happier.

Boys have a biological need for at least four recesses a day. Yet in public schools, recess or physical education is less frequent than it was thirty years ago. This makes no sense to me. As American children become fatter and fatter, recess gets shorter and shorter. How can this trend possibly make any sense? Meanwhile, distractions proliferate with computer games replacing hide-and-seek, and online chat rooms substituting for face-to-face relationships. If a boy has homework, chances are he will spend his nights either sitting in front of a computer screen or reading.

If we care about the boys who will become husbands and fathers later on, what is the cure? I wish there were an easy solution. As Americans, we're accustomed to quick fixes and "just add water" remedies. I have little doubt that boys and young men are confused about who they are, for they're also confused about what it means to be a man. They're frustrated by systems that seem to be stacked against them. They're bored in school, bored in church, and ready for someone to help them figure out what to do—before it's too late.

If you're a dad, chances are you're not trying to "fix" your son. He may not be like you, but ideally, you give him latitude to figure out his own interests while gently pushing him into new experiences. Mothers tend to be the "fixers," and this is exactly what young boys do not need. If we want automatons in our society, then keep trying to fix boys. If we want weak husbands or ineffectual fathers, then fixing boys is the answer. They will get the message that they need fixing, and they will take this message into every compartment of their lives, always wondering why they don't measure up.

In education, at home, in private or public school, here are a few suggestions for those who live or work with boys.

1. Stop trying to "fix" or "tame" boys. Stop emotionally neutering them or expecting them to be more like girls.
2. Stop overmedicating them in an effort to control behavioral problems.
3. Provide more time for play.
4. Encourage hands-on learning (using all the senses).
5. Recognize gender bias in education. Speak up when you see it.
6. Recognize learning differences between the sexes. Use more gender-friendly approaches with boys that capture their interest.
7. Recruit more male teachers in church education programs.
8. Ask other men to become proactive in helping mentor your son.
9. Build family activity time into every day (which means turning off computers, televisions, music, or other electronic distractions).
10. Use home-education techniques that work with boys. Educational videos, field trips, and hikes are good learning tools.

Caught in the Cross Fire
Teenage Boys Who Won't Grow Up

IT WAS stifling hot. I was sixteen years old and had just completed my sophomore year of high school. I was working with my friend Gene in a trucking yard in downtown Los Angeles, loading forty-foot trailers in the summer! The metal on the inside walls of the trailer was so hot I would burn my hand if I touched them. The sweat poured off our heads as if our craniums had sprung a leak. Our job was to load Mattel toys, tools, and anything else the owner wanted crammed inside the container. Hour after miserable hour, day after day, we worked—for a paltry $1.65 an hour. But it was work. And for a teenage boy, work was good. It meant freedom in some way I can't explain today. In some validating way, we always felt good when the day was over. We felt even better when we cashed our checks. It paid for our gas, our insurance, and for repairs on cars that should have gone to the scrap yard years before.

On one of those boiling summer days, I was tossing heavy boxes to Gene. I was in overdrive and started chucking those boxes like bullets in his direction. The more he complained, the faster I catapulted the heavy boxes toward him. It was fun, in a sadistic sort of way. Neither one of us thought about how this might end, of course; teenagers don't. Finally, Gene had all he was going to take from me, so boxes started coming back in my direction at lightning speed. You get the picture. (Now you know who handles the boxes with the "Fragile" stickers!) Before long, boxes started breaking open and tools littered the floor of the container. Sweat continued to flow as our faces grew red and our frustration mounted. There we were, two exhausted and overworked teenage boys, creating conflict for ourselves. What was the outcome? Gene and I finally put down the boxes and went at each other like a couple of Greco-Roman wrestlers. I know it was stupid. Fortunately, the boss must have seen his trailer swaying back and forth, so he came out and put an end to our foolishness. And despite our ridiculous clash of the Titans, Gene and I left that day as friends, and we remain friends to this day.

In fact, today Gene says, "I remember that day in the tractor-trailer, sweating like horses, and you upping the volume with each toss. We were lucky we didn't suffer from heat stroke." The important point of this story is what Gene says next, something that is lost on many parents and teenage boys today: "Our kids don't have the reference because they get pocket money in easier ways. Having the responsibility of gainful employment is good for the overall development of adolescents. Our kids' generation seems to miss that."

When I was a teenager, we worked our tails off during the summer. It was good for us. We learned the importance of taking responsibility for what little our parents made us pay for, mainly our transportation and dates with girls. Our work had nothing to do with our parents' socioeconomic status. I remember painting fences, trimming trees, washing windows, taking out trash, and organizing the garage. After school—that's after football practice in the fall or track practice in the spring—I had a regular job. And I don't remember complaining, although I'm sure I did.

Each man has a different story to tell about his first job. If you're an adult male, you know your own story. Those of us who develop a healthy work ethic generally develop it as young boys or during our teenage years—mowing lawns, painting, or working at the local fast-food restaurant. But here's the catch. Many teenage boys today are underachieving. They're discontent with just any job. They want a "good job," whatever that means to them. Here is another observation about today's teenage boys. They're growing up slower than in previous generations, but I don't mean in a physical sense. Generally, they're slow to develop emotionally and lack the maturity of previous generations. Words like commitment, responsibility, consequences, boundaries, and sacrifice are unpopular with their age group. Fathers tell their sons, "You can be anything you want," but that's a lie; they can't. Sure, opportunity abounds, but it can be too much of a good thing. Teenagers are overwhelmed with choices. Parents think that by having more choices, their sons are better off, that there is an intrinsic goodness to variety. Society has got us believing that this is the right of all Americans, but that's nonsense. Having too many choices breeds confusion. Just walk down the cereal aisle of your grocery store, and you'll know what I'm talking about. In previous generations, boys had responsibilities. They were part of a team called "family." Each member of the family contributed to the success of the unit. This concept seems lost today. Perhaps it has to do with the ever-changing structure of the family or the individualism that has run amuck in our society. Whatever the reason, it's not good news for families in general or for teenage boys in particular.

In the previous chapter, we looked at the messages boys receive during their elementary years—especially in education. In the remainder of this chapter, we will look at how sociological changes and messages have fostered greater confusion for teenage boys.

The Pursuit of Happiness

Our present culture deifies happiness and choice above all else, and it's ruining boys and men alike. We're drunk on materialism, suffering from sensual overload, and lost to what really matters. We're a Matrix-driven culture where marketing supplants truth, self triumphs over sacrifice, and image is everything. But many of us simply cannot see it. And this blindness is more than cultural myopia; it's self-deception. We want to believe the untruths because they feed us in ways that soothe our flesh, our ego, our security.

Youth are bent on the vague notion of "finding themselves," which is the exact opposite of what Christ taught about dying to self. They stimulate themselves into a stupor, and then wonder why they're so unhappy. Yet there's no long-term satisfaction. If mere desire equals personal right, teenage boys feel a *right* to feed their senses. Why not? In a society whose mantra is, "If it makes you happy, do it," why should we expect teenage boys to act any differently?

It's easy for mothers of teenage sons to fall into this happiness trap by failing to hold their ground. Some dads do it too, but because mothers are nurturers, they often give in when a teenage boy most needs them *not* to give in. In the end, boys do not learn to respect a parent who gives in to their every desire. They respect boundaries. They want limits, though they will never tell you this. And they need them. An angry, strong-willed boy can be an intimidating force to a mother, and she may give in because the battle is too tiring. Either way, she does the boy a disservice by reinforcing his narcissistic tendencies and his sense of entitlement.

I have never doubted the importance of establishing and maintaining boundaries in the lives of boys. While employed as a psychosocial rehabilitation specialist, I had an encounter that reinforced those beliefs. I was working with half a dozen boys who had just been in the pool at a health club in town. All but one were in the process of getting dressed and ready to leave. The exception was a seven-year-old boy who was running naked around the locker room, rubbing his genitals on the other boys. It was a terribly uncomfortable situation, and the boys didn't know what to do or how to handle it. On three separate occasions I told this pint-sized streaker to stop, that his behavior was inappropriate.

Finally, I had to grab him from behind and insist that he stop. I then waited until he finished getting dressed as the other boys left. On the way out, something quite unexpected occurred. The boy locked onto my leg and hugged me in an affectionate though nonsexual way. My emotions were bouncing back and forth between frustration and compassion, as I realized this boy was expressing his gratitude at the fact that I had cared enough to set and maintain boundaries. Boys, including teenagers, interpret reasonable boundaries as a parent's (or any other authority figure's) way of expressing love. When we fail to do that and instead give into everything they think they want or need, we create narcissistic sons and men.

Genuine happiness has limits. It comes not from indulging in the material but from giving ourselves away for others. It's found in the investments we make to bless others. The concept is a paradox, and it's precisely what teenage boys need to hear. If they don't, how can we expect them to grow up to take responsibility for a wife, family, or job? They may do it for a while, but once the liabilities outweigh the benefits, they won't have the character to hang in there. Character is what happens when a boy places his will and his happiness below the needs of others. It's what happens when immediate gratification is placed in check.

In the movie, *The Emperor's Club*, actor Kevin Kline plays a teacher at a prestigious school in the Northeast. At the end of the movie, twenty-five years after his students grew into successful men—educators, politicians, businessmen—Kline realizes the one boy who has failed the most is the one he worked the hardest to save. Although a multimillionaire, the man is still cutting corners in life to get what he wants. In reflection, Kline says, "A man's character is his fate . . . The worth of a life is not determined by a single failure or a solitary success."

Boys will fail, and often do. It's part of growing up. The best men throughout history failed in some way. As a matter of fact, teenage boys *need* to fail. It's through failure that the character finds its most fertile soil. Boys also need to risk. The risk, however, must take on healthy qualities rather than self-destructive ones. Many teenage boys want to have fun, but they don't want to grow up. Maybe it's fear. Maybe it's too many options. Maybe it's lack of direction. Whatever it is, boys will inevitably choose the easy road if they aren't pushed into the next phase of life.

It's less frightening to stay in childhood—to keep having fun. A male friend of mine refers to these boys as being in "womb lock"—a good metaphor for boys who don't want to leave their comfortable surroundings. They want to remain in a cocoon of safety. A mother must not let this happen if she cares about her son's future as a man. A healthy mother-son bond is not about her emotional needs; it's about his. If a boy stays in this protective place, he will fall farther behind boys who break free earlier. Teenagers must learn to experience the world as God meant it to be, in all its fullness and risk and scariness. Adventure helps prepare boys for this breaking away, for it gives them—especially in their teenage years—the confidence to launch out into the world on their own.

As we explore some of the reasons teenage boys are struggling, it helps to look beneath the surface at some of the damaging messages and faulty ideas that influence their thinking. Before we look at these issues more closely, let's find out what's happening to these boys within our culture.

An Endangered Tribe

By inadvertently robbing boys of their expressiveness and trying to tame them, society has put them in an almost impossible situation, expecting them to become responsible men without being properly trained or prepared to do so. Teens feel this pressure to become something they sense they're ill-equipped to be. Consequently, some boys act up while, conversely, others become victims of those who act up. Lost boys act up because they want and need attention. They want to know where they fit in the world—especially the world of other men.

In my midtwenties, I volunteered at several adolescent boys' placement centers in and around Los Angeles. One of these was Camp Carl Holton, an L.A. County Juvenile Detention Center hidden in the hills of the San Fernando Valley. There were some tough kids there. A few were gang members—blacks, whites, and Latinos. I spent nearly every week there for two years and learned more than I ever wanted to know about the habits and hang-ups of this subculture. During the time at Holton, I worked with Steve, a fifteen-year-old who couldn't stay out of trouble. After his release, Steve came to live with me and began making responsible choices with his life. What struck me most about Steve was that he was a good kid, though he came from a messed-up family—as many adolescents do today. We know that children—both boys and girls—from fatherless homes are five times more likely to commit suicide, thirty-two times more likely to run away, and twenty times more likely to end up in prison. But what about boys specifically?

According to Dan Kindlon and Michael Thompson in their book, *Raising Cain*, boys commit 95 percent of juvenile homicides. They're responsible for four out of five crimes that end up in juvenile court. They account for almost nine out of ten alcohol and drug law violations. Meanwhile, suicide is the third leading cause of death among boys in their mid to late teens. The authors say the inner turmoil in boys is expressed in academic failure, depression, drug addiction, alcoholism, troubled relationships, or delinquency.[1] Depression, in particular, is a serious problem among boys, often leading to substance abuse. Boys who are under stress are at increased risk for depression. And the stressors for boys are significant, especially with so many growing up without an emotionally solid male in their lives. This is not a pretty picture of where teenage boys are in today's society.

In my book, *Teach Your Children Well*, I explain the importance of fathers in the lives of their sons. Yet, sadly, the role of fathers in our society has been minimized, marginalized, and degraded. Using research by David Popenoe and others, here's a condensed version of what I say about this topic in my book.

The way fathers play with their children impacts everything from management of emotions to intelligence and academic achievement. Fathers tend to stress competition, challenge, initiative, risk-taking, and independence. The involvement of a father in the life of a child is also linked to better verbal communication and problem-solving skills.[2] Fathers teach their sons to make it in the world. Adolescent boys know this intuitively. If a father is absent or unwilling to fill this role, a boy is likely to flounder until he figures it out on his own, often drawing wrong conclusions. Most likely, he will bounce in and out of jobs or relationships. He may wonder what's wrong with everyone else and never look inside himself.

As for Steve, he ended up back in prison—this time in an adult facility. It broke my heart because I knew his heart was tender. He had no business in an adult facility, but there he was—a victim of his own poor choices and those of the parents who failed him. I see many adolescent boys like Steve who have no limits or boundaries. They don't know how to grow up. They have no role model for the journey into adulthood. In his book, *A Boy's Passage*, Brian Molitor argues for the importance of rites of passage for adolescent males. "In an attempt to compensate for the lack of a transitional event, some teens unknowingly create their own rites of passage by resorting to violence, drugs, alcohol or sexual conquest to try to make their transition into adulthood."[3]

Lost, hurting boys become hurting, angry men. Is this what our society wants to foster? With our worldview compass set on personal happiness for its own sake, it's no wonder responsibility and commitment fall to the wayside. These qualities fall victim to what former Supreme Court nominee Robert Bork called personal license and social disorder. As adolescent boys grow into angry men, they do not view the women in their lives with respect. Rather, they abuse them—not just in a physical sense, but also by using them for their own sexual or emotional needs before discarding them for their next fix. This cyclical madness deepens the chasm between the sexes, intensifies the hurt, furthers cynicism, and generates fear of attachment (a necessary ingredient in healthy relationships).

If young boys need to express themselves through physical challenge, play, or adventure, adolescent boys with unresolved issues will express themselves physically through aggression. In the former, the physicality is a positive and necessary expression that is too often stifled. In the latter, the physicality is a negative expression that wreaks havoc on society through violent crime and the victimization of women. It is, in the final analysis, symptomatic of larger social and spiritual issues that diminish marriage, weaken men, and encourage self-fulfillment as an end in itself.

The Messages and the Challenges for Boys

In his autobiography, *On My Honor*, former attorney general John Ashcroft said, "When a mission defines who you are, there is no you when the mission dies."[4] Many boys and men don't know what their mission is, and this invariably places them at a crossroads. Anyone who has stood at a crossroad knows a choice must be made. Some adolescent boys make the wrong choice, while others delay making critical decisions because they lack direction and guidance.

Former football great Barry Sanders grasped the importance of mission and identity early on. Sanders was no stranger to awards and accolades. He was voted high school player of the year in 1986; made the College All-American Team in 1988; won the Walter Camp Trophy, the Maxwell Award, and the Heisman Trophy in 1988; and in his first year as a Detroit Lion, went to the Pro Bowl and was named Rookie of the Year in 1989. With all those credits to his name, you'd think his personal identity and mission would center around football. But when asked how he felt about winning the Heisman Trophy, Sanders said, "It's a wonderful thing to achieve success in your chosen sport. But the real test comes when things get tough and you have to find out who you are away from that sport."[5] A wise statement from one so young—and a rare statement as well, since few males understand this great truth at such a tender age.

As James Dobson observes, "Boys are in trouble today primarily because their parents, and especially their dads, are distracted, over-worked, harassed, exhausted, disinterested, chemically dependent, divorced, or simply unable to cope . . . all other problems plaguing young males flow from (or relate to) these facts of life in the twenty-first century."[6]

Following are ten of the primary challenges faced by adolescent boys today, each of which I will briefly address.

1. Materialism
2. Narcissism
3. Spiritual irrelevance
4. Uncertainty
5. Sexuality and experimentation
6. Rejection and disappointment

7. Self-medication
8. Libertine worldview shaped by their education and the media
9. Masculine diminishment
10. Fear, anger, and violence

Materialism is no less a destructive force than any other false religious belief system. As westerners accustomed to having so much of everything, we just can't see our own overindulgence. If we do see it, we somehow equate it to God's favorable disposition toward us. This is twisted thinking. Commercial forces, marketing, greed—each combine to stir up a simmering dissatisfaction. If a person can't get what he wants through legitimate means, he lies, cheats, steals, or manipulates to get it. The commercial messages are everywhere, and they're far more sophisticated than ever. Boys are easy prey to their seduction. Consider this astonishing statistic. On the Internet alone, marketers send about 7.3 billion messages . . . a day.[7] My guess is this number is actually higher.

Perhaps you're thinking, so what? What difference does this make? It does matter, and it does make a difference because too many options mean too many decisions. And too many decisions place us on mental overload, a problem that is out of hand today. Do we really need 150 channels at our fingertips? And yet, along with everything else these boys must contend with, they feel this pressure of too many choices. As mentioned earlier, they're afraid to make a decision because they might make the wrong one. And making the wrong decision may influence how they feel now, as well as their future happiness or lack of contentment. Then what?

The goal of a materialistic culture is to keep its people in a state of dissatisfaction. This has many offshoots, but at least one is the compulsive comparison with what others have—and that's called covetousness. These comparisons lead to a sense of relative deprivation when we look with envy on those who have more than we do. This leads to a natural progression toward ingratitude, and this lack of thankfulness is the curse of a culture that places a greater value on things and lesser emphasis on character.

Narcissism finds fertile ground in a materialistic, me-centered culture. Altruism and self-sacrifice are undervalued. How do boys become self-centered? When their parents give them just about anything they want. These boys then develop an attitude of entitlement, always expecting parents to bail them out or buy them what they think they need. Affluence encourages this faulty attitude. Parents who are overworked, insecure, or too busy often substitute money or experiences for real time spent with their boys. Perhaps it's induced by guilt or by what they see other parents doing. The reason isn't important. What is important is that it harms boys who need boundaries. The late author, Allan Bloom, says about self-centeredness, "The resulting inevitable individualism, endemic to our regime, has been reinforced by another unintended and unexpected development, the decline of the family."[8]

Spiritual irrelevance is a two-sided coin. First, overindulgence in a fast-paced, visually appealing, media-saturated culture makes it difficult to keep a boy's attention. Boys need downtime. They need time away from computers, phones, games, TV, or other distractions, including peers. Our culture has become addicted to images and sounds. They have forgotten (if they ever knew) about quiet, about stillness, about meditation. Our boys' tolerance for under-stimulation is low. Second, these truths make it increasingly difficult to hold a boy's focus. Churches face unprecedented challenges to keep the attention of boys living in a hyper-stimulated culture. Simply put, fathers will lose their sons to the world if the world does a better job of capturing their attention. They will also lose them if we do a poor job of establishing and maintaining boundaries in the home.

Uncertainty has always been a challenge. Yet something is different about it today. We have an intuitive sense that the world is teetering on the edge. It isn't just the fear of terror; it's a general dread that natural resources, overpopulation, globalization, and the lethality of weaponry can change the world as we know it. We're losing open spaces. Frontiers are dwindling. I could go on, but you get the point. Uncertainty makes decision making more difficult, and boys feel this. What should I do? How do I achieve success? What *is* success? Even definitions of reality are changing. Have you ever wondered why Jesus prefaced many of his statements with "fear not"? God understands our humanness. He understands our fears, our anxiety. It's our human tendency to delay major decisions when the choices are unclear and the outcomes impossible to predict.

Sexuality and experimentation are as big a temptation as ever. The double standard that said boys could be sexually promiscuous but girls couldn't is long gone. Now, girls are often the aggressors, and pornography is available in the privacy of a boy's bedroom (if parents allow Internet access there). The new rules encourage experimentation—homosexual, group sex, bisexual, heterosexual—it doesn't matter, since you won't be judged. Just try it once. The pressure is there. Weak boys find it difficult to stand on their own. Fathers must set the standard and explain how bucking the mores of a sexualized society is more emotionally and spiritually intelligent than succumbing to them. Why should a boy grow up if he can get everything he wants without taking responsibility? Today he can have sex without commitment, sex without disease (if he's very careful), and sex without financial obligation (if he's smart).

Rejection and disappointment are part of becoming a man. Boys who are accustomed to hearing yes are not prepared when the world serves up a no. If they have been spoiled and pampered, and most are today, they will delay their development when times get hard. Fathers must prepare their sons for real life, not for painless life. Hardships will come. Jobs will be lost, girls will turn away, friends will let us down, and money will be tight. This is life. One of my sons once told me about how another guy was flirting with the girl my son was talking to in a restaurant, and it made my son mad. I probed further to ask how he really felt—beyond mad. He admitted he felt rejected. I recognized that my son had sustained a wound, so I put my hand on his shoulder and said, "Welcome to the world of men!" It happens, and the earlier boys recognize the wounds of rejection and disappointment, the less likely they will be to allow these wounds to put them in deep-freeze.

Self-medication occurs when a boy thinks his wounds are too much to handle. He will look for ways to "check out" from reality, and he often does this with drugs, alcohol, or tobacco. The driving forces for this self-destructive behavior could be family wounds, low self-esteem, laziness, or fear. While some of these boys are prodigals trying to make sense of the world, others are not getting their lives back on track at all. They refuse to grow up because it's no fun, too hard, or they're caught in a trap and don't know how to get out. Many give in to their pain and develop a lifestyle that makes sense only to themselves and a cadre of dysfunctional pals. They live spontaneously for the moment. The older a boy-man gets without dealing with his addictions, the more he comes to accept them as his own. He embraces them. He identifies with them. They become who he is, or at least, who he sees himself as being. The self-medication prevents a boy from making the break from childhood into manhood.

The libertine worldview is nothing new. After the influence of the family, the media and education are the next two most influential forces in the life of a boy. Both of these institutions are overwhelmingly liberal in their moral outlook on the world today. Attorney David French wrote about the bias in public education, saying, "The law allows the liberal to indoctrinate while sometimes denying Christians even the opportunity to persuade . . . American public and private colleges have taken it

upon themselves to teach your children a particular worldview—
a worldview that is diametrically opposed to much of the
Bible."[9] Meanwhile, Harvard graduate and writer William
Proctor doesn't even believe media objectivity is possible. In reference to the *New York Times*, Proctor said, "It is not a bastion
of unbiased, objective news coverage. Instead, all evidence points
toward an organization that sees itself as the primary guardian
of the great worldview and what the paper regards as a virtually
infallible set of guiding truths that demand to be disseminated
widely and promoted ardently."[10]

*The diminishment of masculinity is now a part of today's
society.* Boys are less likely to want to grow up if being a man
carries negative baggage or stigma. They're damned if they do
and damned if they don't, so they avoid it. In the rush to create
a culture of sameness, society educates the natural aggressiveness out of boys. The Greeks coined the term *stigma*, and the
idea behind it was to brand, cut, or otherwise mark a person's
body so others knew that person was a slave, criminal, or trai-
tor. While we don't physically brand people in our culture, social
stigma is every bit as real. Stigma can be any attribute that is
deeply discrediting and makes a person feel inferior or like he's
not good enough or he doesn't measure up. As masculine roles
and definitions change, boys will need better definitions about
what it means to be a man. Fathers must take the lead in this
important transition by modeling and educating about maleness.

Fear, anger, and violence have been part of the male experience since Cain and Abel. To the extent that teenage boys and
young men feel unsure about themselves, the level of anger, violence, or passivity increases. Fear, rejection, shame, pain—these
all trigger anger, and anger is the precursor to violence. In a society that worships violent images, men with unresolved frustration will increasingly act out on their misplaced expectations.
Paradoxically, our society has been sowing the seeds of anger
and violence in men for decades. Simultaneously, we preach

about respect for women and boundaries in dating relationships. We keep sending mixed messages to boys and men, and then expect them to act in ways we deem civil. Some men respond to this by becoming passive, while others lash out. Certainly, boys need limits, and they need ways to express their frustration. They need rules that are clear, rules that don't change, rules that make sense.

Teenage boys in our culture are struggling to understand their role in the world. They're struggling to understand themselves, though they may not be aware of it. Christian parents can help their teenage sons recognize the confusing messages from education and the media. Mothers must learn to step back, allowing their husbands to take the lead in the waning days of a son's transition into adulthood. Fathers must step up to their responsibility, or sons will find their own way, and this is rarely a good thing.

Finding Family
The Search to Belong

MIKE IS a quiet twenty-eight-year-old with a good job and a terrific girlfriend named Jessica. They love each other, or so they say. Both attend the same church and share the same Christian faith, but something is wrong. The relationship is stuck in neutral at a time when it ought to be growing. Jessica can't understand why Mike won't ask her to marry him, but she refuses to be a nag; it's against her nature. At twenty-seven, she is patient, kind, pretty, and confused. "We have talked about marriage, and Mike agrees that one day he will ask me to marry him," says Jessica. "I just don't know what's taking him so long. What is he waiting for?"

Indeed, what is Mike waiting for? When will he be ready? How will he know when he's ready? For men like Mike, fear is pervasive, paralyzing them into inaction. What makes them afraid? They aren't sure. These twentysomething and even thirty-something men are not taking the route of their fathers. Instead, they're delaying marriage more than any previous generation. They're waiting, and waiting, until the women in their lives get tired of it. Who hasn't heard women talk about how men can't commit to anything? These angst-ridden women are right; men fear commitment if it means the kind of relationship failures many of them saw while growing up. They have seen bad marriages, and some men are asking themselves, "Who needs this?" But it's more than just having poor conjugal role models. Even young men from solid families with good role models are choosing to delay marriage and family life.

In 1960, the average age of a groom was twenty-three. Today, it's nearly twenty-seven. That men and women are delaying marriage is not in question. What is in question is *why* they're delaying. In his book, *Mismatch*, political scientist Andrew Hacker explains it this way: "Young people now want a prolonged period of freedom before tying a legal knot. They say they don't feel ready for marriage, which is essentially another way of saying that they look forward to the excitement of independent living. They also feel less pressured to marry because others think they should."[1]

Women like Jessica feel stuck in cultural quicksand. They want to move forward in their relationships, but the men in their lives don't seem to budge. These women fear that if they push too hard, he will leave. If they just do nothing, he will never make up his mind. Sound familiar? We live in a culture where we discard relationships like day-old newspapers. No wonder women are confused about their men. They ask themselves just how much time they should invest in a man who can't seem to make up his mind. And it's a fair question.

In previous eras, men knew exactly what was expected of them. Whether you agree or disagree with traditional male or female roles is not the issue. What *is* the issue is how men perceive their roles today. I use the word *perceive* because that's all many men have to grab a hold of, and the definitions are increasingly elusive. When it comes to committing to serious relationships, men often delay as long as they can. Some do so for fear they will end up in miserable relationships. Others simply fear commitment. Some want to squeeze the last vestiges of twilight from their self-centered lives. Still others fear something more; they feel unworthy and underprepared.

Meanwhile, women like Jessica wait, hoping the men in their lives will suddenly grow some courage and take a leap of faith.

Stuck in Neutral: Why Young Men Postpone Relationships

We have already talked about why some men freeze up when trying to make major decisions in their lives: too many choices equal confusion, and confusion leads to delay. Better to delay than to make the wrong choice. We've all seen men miss great opportunities on a house, car, or relationship because they need time to think it over. This "failure" serves to reinforce an underlying feeling of panic, a sense of dread that comes when the stakes are high. And nowhere are the stakes as high as in marriage relationships.

Freedom of choice in our consumer-oriented culture has given way to an unintended, though very real, effect. We don't just suffer from information overload; we suffer from information trauma. Men are in a collective state of shock, afraid to make the wrong decision. When it comes to marriage, they want to be sure. They want to keep their options open, always wondering if this is the best deal they can get. Yet, if you ask most young men about when they'll be sure or what ingredients have to fall into place to help them become surer, they can't give a good answer. Sure, some will say they want a better job, more money in the bank, a house, or whatever. But these are smokescreens that point more to their own narcissism than to legitimate or rational reasons.

Young men delay commitment to marriage for many reasons, but mostly from fear (loss of independence or worry about finding the right person). Many don't want to lose their free-dom (selfishness) or want their financial/vocational life in order (security). Let's take a closer look at several of these contribut-ing factors.

The fear of messing up keeps men indecisive. Fear, insecu-rity, lack of self-esteem—these are close cousins. A boy who doesn't develop self-esteem in his early years will often avoid tough decisions later on or delay them as long as possible. Men fear commitment in some cases because they fear failure. To fail is to reinforce an already fragile ego, often delayed in its devel-opment due to masculine bewilderment. Self-esteem is a by-product of adventure, of risk, of accomplishment or expertise, of real-life experience. A mother who disallows this in a boy inadvertently trains him to avoid risk later on.

Susan is a thirty-five-year-old widowed mother with two boys—but she gets it. With her youngest son away on an overnight trip, she decided to do something fun with her thirteen-year-old. "The evening didn't go as planned," she explained, "but we did stop by a place that has go-carts. I bought him a ticket, and he climbed behind the wheel of a manly racecar. Several other tough-looking guys climbed into their own cars, and I thought my son would choke in their fumes until the end. I watched and even prayed that night over these very issues: 'God, am I doing it right? Will he be OK?' As I prayed, my son pulled ahead. Eventually, he lapped everyone in that race. He came out beaming, and I felt God had answered my prayer."

Perhaps God did answer Susan's prayer. She set him up for future success by allowing her son to take a risk. Boys do not become men through singular experiences, yet these seemingly simple "successes" are more meaningful than we think.

Past failure, even in relationships, is no predictor of future failure. Young men often find it easier to give up, reorienting their internal compass to a lower common denominator. Their new benchmark for success has fewer risks. It's a form of surrender. Later in life, these men are never completely fulfilled and don't know why. They may feel it in their guts, but acknowledging they have capitulated to their fear is too much for most men to bear. They wonder, "Could I have become more?" This question nags at the gates of their soul. It grates on them until at midlife they accept their lives as the status quo or journey into the unknown. To do the latter requires them to muster every ounce of courage, and often they go about it the wrong way.

Postmodern sexual values make singleness easier. It's no secret that today's young men can get their sexual needs met without long-term commitment. This doesn't mean a man in his twenties or early thirties will never marry; it just means he's not in the same hormone-induced rush to do so as men were in previous generations. Nor do cultural mores demand abstinence as in the past. This places more pressure on unmarried men, even those with vibrant faith and strong character.

A smorgasbord of birth-control options (including abortion) makes sex less risky (except for sexually transmitted diseases). Women, presumably liberated from the old Victorian values, now engage in sex-for-fun rather than sex-for-relationship. By glamorizing casual sex, some believe that "hooking up" is an innocuous way of meeting their needs for temporary companionship and physical release. The biblical paradigm for intercourse is about two people becoming one flesh. This concept is deeper than the physical act; it forges an emotional-spiritual connection as well. Meanwhile, the social acceptance of sex outside of marriage places a greater burden on young Christian men who are no less sexually inclined than men who have no faith at all. Many unmarried men and women delay marriage because the sexual benefits once associated with a legal marriage are no longer an issue, at least from the standpoint of the stigma that once served as a regulator on sexual activity. Though it seems logical to "test drive" relationships before marriage, the preponderance of research shows that couples who live together beforehand have higher rates of divorce (at about 60 percent) than those who do not live together first.

Men enjoy their freedom and equate it with happiness. Freedom without responsibility is a dead end. Men interpret freedom as doing anything they want, anytime they want, however they want. This is another false belief, fostered by a culture drenched in rights but adrift of responsibilities. Young men want to do more than sow their wild oats. They don't want to give up a lifestyle that offers variety, limited accountability, the opportunity to come and go as they please, and a chance to extend an already overextended boyhood. In other words, there is little or no outside pressure to settle down as there once was. Author and scientist Andrew Hacker observes, "Now you have guys who are 35-year-old seventeen year olds . . . adolescence lasts until 25 or 40 now."[2] Not surprisingly, the fixation on self-pleasure is detrimental to a healthy marriage.

The key to a successful marriage, according to David Blankenhorn in *Fatherlessness in America*, is harnessing individual happiness with collective well-being.[3] While this may be true, how does a young man interpret a selfless concept like collective well-being when he has been saturated with messages to "do your own thing"? These mixed signals create what social scientists refer to as cognitive dissonance. To delay gratification for the sake of community requires character, and character is dreadfully elusive in our rights-dominated culture. We no longer see the death to self and its urges as virtuous. Instead, we see the delay of gratification as an unnecessary intrusion that sets off an over-active superego (the Bible calls it conscience). The "live for the moment" philosophy in postmodern culture encourages us to drown the conscience in a sea of questionable experience, reasoning that experience is better than inexperience since it enhances our ability to make informed choices. Conversely, it often dulls the conscience and makes moral decision making more problematic, which leads to confusion and finally to unhappiness.

Before a boy can become a man, according to Robert Bly, something infantile must die in him. Bly believes the warrior inside the American male has become weak in recent years, and these weaknesses contribute to a lack of boundaries . . . naiveté.[4] If contemporary society encourages women to be warriors, it discourages warriorhood in boys and men. The fading of the warrior will lead to the collapse of civilized society. If boys are lost and confused, then young men in their twenties and thirties are even farther down the path to lostness. They may cloak their lostness in pursuit of pleasure or things, but these are only tiny bandages over gaping emotional wounds.

Men want to have their ducks in a row. Jason is thirty-two years old, college-educated, has a good job, and enjoys the out-doors. He has dabbled in relationships but doesn't want to get serious until he has plenty of money in the bank, his car paid off, and enough money to buy a house. Many of today's pre-marital men want to start married life standing on second base. They want to skip ahead, as if pulling the Monopoly card that invites them to pass *Go* and collect $200.

Couples who married in earlier generations understood that life together would be a journey. They understood that having it all figured out ahead of time made their journey less about the collective *them* and more about the individual *I*. There is a mercurial quality to every relationship. It's an ever-growing, ever-changing organism. The successful marriage manages change, seasons of life, conflict, and unavoidable expectations. In other words, couples grow together, more into *we* and less into *me*. This growth never precludes individuality, expression, opinion, or difference. What it does is grow linearly—toward a common goal.

This is not to say men should rush into marriage and ignore obvious areas of potential or real contention. But men in their early adult years increasingly want the material benefits their parents worked decades to attain. In the minds of these men, marriage is akin to a strategic move on a chessboard, rather than a leap of faith into an unknown adventure.

Men don't want to repeat the same mistakes they saw growing up. This excuse is a paradox but an understandable one. Most men want to marry, and they understand that to do so means they have to settle down. Some men use poor role models (usually their parents or other close family members) as examples of how their marriage will *never* be.

It's typical for some men to seek a woman with qualities similar to their own mother. They don't think about it at the time, but it happens. This means the likelihood of projecting subconscious expectations on their spouse are extremely high. Similarly, women often marry a man and expect him to be like their father. After all, their father (if they had one around) is the one man, for better or worse, from which women learn about masculinity. The pattern of masculine "truth" impressed upon women by their father is so ingrained that most women find it difficult, if not impossible, to alter their definition of reality or to accommodate the differences in their mate.

The paradox is that when it comes to relationships, most men are truly optimistic. They believe they'll duck the divorce bullet and live happily ever after. Yet, as recent statistics from George Barna show, even Christian marriages fail at an astonishingly high rate. Young men often forego marriage because they do not know what a good marriage looks like. Instead of jumping into uncharted relationship territory, they simply wait. This response is one of fear, for most men desperately want to succeed in their relationships. Some wonder if they have what it takes to make it through to the end. Those who do often find women who are genuine helpers, encouragers, friends, and champions.

Many men are emotionally retarded. A recent study found the majority of boys ages thirteen to sixteen (85 percent) say they watch "youth comedies." Since teens are the primary target of these shows, the producers and advertisers are happy about it. What they didn't expect is that men ages twenty-one to twenty-five also watch the *same* youth comedies (84 percent).[5] The message is clear—not much maturity is happening in men between their late teen years and their midtwenties.

Emotional intelligence is a broad term. I define it as encompassing mental acuity, spiritual passion, social connectedness, emotional vulnerability, physical activity, and intellectual development. An emotional delay is largely the result of a society that does not demand that its men grow up. Many men and boys, particularly those growing up during the affluent '90s, have had it too easy. The same can be said, though less so, for boys and men growing up as part of the Baby Boom generation (born 1946–1962). Men rarely grow up emotionally without encountering some form of hardship. Difficulty, crisis, challenge—these offer opportunity for character development. Boys and men have too many choices and far too few afflictions. Character develops from the latter, while emotional handicaps accrue from the former.

I mentioned in Chapter 2 that men like Joseph and King David found their character through difficulty. I challenge you to find a single well-known biblical character who did not face his or her struggles. Noah, Abraham, Queen Esther, Nehemiah, Gideon, Peter, Paul—each came face-to-face with tough, if not nearly impossible, circumstances. In today's world, "tough" is not having cable TV, enough money for a new motorcycle, or the right brand of pants. Our definitions of hardship pale in comparison to generations past, and until men develop character, they will be ill-suited and underprepared for serious relationships.

How Marriage Changes Men

I can speak from experience. When I married in my midtwenties, something inside me changed. Life became more serious. It wasn't just about me anymore, and that meant a more serious effort to complete my education. I also began taking fewer risks.

Just months before I married, I traveled to Mexico with two friends to climb Popocatepetl, a nearly 18,000-foot volcano. Unlike other climbs I had done in the past, I thought more consciously about the risks involved. After that trip, I began to place high-risk ventures on the back burner for a while.

While marriage may not exactly tame men, it does redirect their priorities—or ought to. A previously self-centered man begins to think outside of himself, becoming other-focused for a change. One side effect for those delaying marriage an extra ten years is that autonomy increases independence. To the extent that men are used to being independent, they find it more difficult to settle down, to become less selfish. Selfishness and success in marriage are not a good mix if a couple wants their marriage to work. Men should not get married until they understand the necessity of being faithful, committed, and selfless.

Marriage changes men in another way. It harnesses their sexual energy and allows them to commit to a purpose greater than themselves. Most men want this; most men need this, and our culture depends upon it. Understandably, some men are never able or willing to make the transition out of their boyhood immaturity, and the women who marry these men soon regret it. The men who cling to childhood while trying to become successful husbands or fathers are headed for trouble. It doesn't work. This attempt to walk the fence is a by-product of a rights-dominated, fun-seeking, affluent culture, and it's counterproductive to vibrant and lasting marriage.

What a man in his twenties and thirties finds difficult to accept is that in making a commitment to a woman, he simultaneously makes a noncommitment to countless other women. It's a demarcation point, a giving up of one thing to get something far greater; and this is precisely why people continue to see marriage as something good. In choosing her, he un-chooses others. It's a form of death, and this produces life. By not choosing other women, he removes himself from the pool of unmarried or uncommitted men.

What difference does this make? It creates greater stability within a society—for women, for children, for the economic well-being of the newly created unit. It places a man in his God-ordained protective role and all that this entails. A family is a microcosm of society, and stability rests in both continuity and commitment.

Has Divorce Really Leveled Off?

The idea that the divorce rate has leveled off is a myth. There are more than a million divorces each year, and the effects on everyone involved remain significant. At first glance, it does look like the divorce rate had started to level off. In the late 1950s, divorce reached its lowest level. Then, during the twenty-year period between 1981 and 2001, the divorce rate dropped again—or so it seemed. While some Christians applauded the good news, others looked deeper, realizing we had not suddenly revalued marriage and commitment while so many other indicators showed just the opposite. So what really happened?

The divorce rate dipped because fewer people were getting married. It's as simple as that. More people are cohabiting, living together without the legal status that marriage confers. Common-law relationships that end in "divorce" never show up in divorce statistics. As Hacker notes, what used to be first marriages are being replaced by periods of time when young people live together. He points out that more than half of Americans are reaching the age of thirty without having been married, and these numbers are growing annually. While statistics are hard to come by, about five million men and women live together as unmarried couples. This is more than the combined populations of Idaho, Montana, Wyoming, and both Dakotas.

Dawn is an attractive thirty-nine-year-old divorced mother with a teenage daughter. She is in a "committed" postmodern relationship with Bob, one of her coworkers who is also divorced and has three children of his own. When I asked Dawn if she has plans to marry Bob, she said, "Oh, no. I have my own place, and he has his. It works better that way." She went on to say she likes her independence and occasional solitude. These serially monogamous relationships are the postmodern equivalent to marriage. They offer sex, companionship, compatibility, and independence. Mostly, they offer seasons of happiness, but very little that lasts. These relationships leave most participants feeling hollow, with the inevitable question, "Is this all there is?" While the question may haunt them, it does little to alter their cyclical behavior.

Thirty-six-year-old Nancy has a more "committed" relationship than Dawn because she actually lives with Jerry. He has helped her raise two sons, and they pool their resources in a mutually beneficial manner—just like a marriage but without the legal status. I asked Nancy the same question: "Do you plan to ever get married?" Her hair-trigger response stunned me. "Heck, no," she said. "What do I need a man for? To ruin my life?" The pain of a past emotionally damaging relationship left its mark on Nancy, though beneath the surface she is kind, caring, and loving. It isn't just men who refuse to get married. In some instances, it's men who want to get married and women who refuse. The lack of pressure *not* to tie the knot leads to coupling behavior for the serially monogamous or hooking up for those who want sex but not the so-called commitment.

Women who make themselves sexually available to men find them less motivated to marry. This effect of sexual and gender liberation is no longer one-sided. Women also want the sex and intimacy without long-term commitment . . . sometimes. The answer to this dilemma, especially for churches, is to maintain reasonable biblical standards for sexual and marital relations, though this is increasingly difficult to do. Many younger men, even those who profess faith, see little reason to delay sexual activity. The social and religious stigma that once regulated sexual behavior is now in tatters. "After all," they reason, "God wants me to be happy."

The picture is even bleaker for young African-American men growing up today. Slavery as a way of separating children from fathers (forced dislocation) set in motion the gradual dysfunction and disequilibrium of the African-American family unit. America continues to reap the tragic consequence of buying and trading black men without thought to the long-term result to their families, their offspring, or their psyche. Black children soon learned to identify with mothers, aunts, or grandmothers, rather than men (fathers). In many Black communities today, the same identification dynamics are at work.

Slavery set into motion the seeds that led to the marginalization of the black male (viewed as less than human, removing him from his roots, his family, and his identity). Many internalized their sense of being unneeded and unnecessary—discarded or torn from the family. Generations of black men have struggled with the kind of marginalization white men are only beginning to experience, but for different reasons. In either case, the long-term results for women, children, and society have been, and will continue to be, tragic. Forced fatherlessness in both the black and white communities is fast becoming volitional fatherlessness. The replacement of men within the home by the feminine influence soon gives way to an institutional replacement (government or social service), thereby adding to the already weakened condition of masculinity and perpetuating a false image of the masculine as God intends. Either way, men feel displaced, and displaced males become angry or beaten men.

When government, regardless of motive, intervenes where fathers, churches, or community should step up, families are torn apart. Throwing government money or services at family problems, except in temporary circumstances, is usually harmful. It doesn't encourage self-sufficiency or responsibility, and it doesn't help self-worth. In fact, it does exactly the opposite: it creates dependency.

A generation of younger men, regardless of their ethnicity, is caught in a double bind about family and relationships. Either they question their fitness as potential men and fathers, or they're traumatized by their own childhood. In his book, *It's Not About the Bike*, Tour de France winner Lance Armstrong unleashes the hurt of a generation: "I never knew my so-called father. Just because he provided the DNA that made me doesn't make him my father, and as far as I'm concerned, there is nothing between us, absolutely no connection. I have no idea who he is, what he likes or dislikes. Before last year, I never knew where he lived or worked. I never asked . . . the thing is, I don't care."[6]

A generation of young men of marrying age is lost and confused. These men may want to be good husbands and fathers, but they don't know how to begin. If they take their cues from popular culture, they will fail—just like many of their fathers did. They will leave angry men like Lance Armstrong to figure out what masculinity, commitment, and sacrifice are all about. They may also become overachievers in an attempt to mask their pain, overloading their lives in hope of finding peace. The only way to ease the pain of a hurting generation is in the arms of the Prince of Peace. He came to give life and to give it abundantly, to give it freely. If men wrestle to make it on their own, their collective pain will filter into the next generation. They will stumble into their midlife years as confused as when they were in their twenties and thirties, when they went about trying to find and establish a family of their own.

CHAPTER **6**

Middle-Aged Madness
The Last Stand

IT TOOK him two long, painful years to figure out what to do. They were the toughest years of his life, and now it was decision time. His energy expended, he felt caught in a trap. What would he do? At forty-eight, Jeff felt like an outcast in his own family. He and his wife, Jill, were strangers living under the same roof. Their counselor called it living "parallel lives."

Jeff and Jill had visited three separate counselors, attended a sixty-hour course on Life Skills, and sought help from pastors and friends. Not one to give up easily, Jeff read the best Christian and secular books about marriage. He prayed and reached out to Jill—all to no avail. His prayers felt like ballistic missiles with faulty electronics. They seemed to miss their target every time, slamming into some remote desert. Where was God?

The tension between Jeff and Jill mounted. It was palpable. Their teenagers felt it. It consumed every spare moment, every waking thought. It caused sleepless nights and stress-filled days. Analytical by nature and a lifelong churchgoer, Jeff knew what was at stake. He knew what it meant to walk out of a marriage. With no movement toward healing and increasing distance between them, Jeff was vulnerable. They had gone from once a week, to once a month, to nothing in the bedroom, and this frustrated him even more. He tried everything he knew to make the marriage work. He *wanted* it to work.

Eventually, Jill uncovered email between Jeff and another woman. Understandably hurt and angry, her anger turned to vindictiveness. Twenty-five years of marriage were unraveling, and they both knew it. Though he had been sexually faithful throughout their marriage, Jeff felt starved for intimacy—sex, friendship, companionship. Jill was either oblivious to his needs or ambivalent. Jeff readily admits his email relationship was not just a mistake—it was a sin. Then he adds, "If your wife doesn't want you to touch her, it leaves a man vulnerable to physical or emotional affirmation from other sources."

Dead Man Walking

After visiting a Christian counselor, Jeff and Jill started remedial separation. He moved out, giving them some emotional breathing room . . . for a while. Jeff stuck it out, asking forgiveness, making personal changes, and asking Jill to dinner on several occasions. The relationship perked ever so briefly and then collapsed into a heap of unresolved emotions. A flood of hurt overwhelmed Jill, who could not let go of her pain. Wrapped tightly in her protective blanket of victimhood, she spilled her guts to anyone who would listen. Jeff felt blindsided. It was as if nothing he said or did made a difference. His discouragement turned to despair. He was losing himself, and he knew it.

Though he understood the oft-quoted biblical admonition to love his wife as Christ loved the church, he was exhausted. He had died a thousand deaths, each time losing a part of who he was as a man. Jeff was dying—emotionally. He could no longer see his way out of his predicament. Even when he took the blame, it didn't seem to be enough to turn the relationship around. Like two war-weary soldiers, Jeff and Jill went to what would be their last counseling session. Jeff sat passively, his strength fading as Jill ticked off fault after fault—seventeen in all. He took notes. Unflinching and detached, his wounds were reopened as one arrow after another penetrated his aching heart. Then it happened. The tears began to flow. The pain, hurt, rejection, and unforgiveness bubbled to the surface and let loose like Old Faithful. He had hoped for something different, for an ounce of empathy or for recognition that their problems were not all his fault. Instead, he found himself overwhelmed, again. He left the counselor's office that day with his mind made up. It was over.

Jeff and Jill's experience is tragic. It could have been different. Outside observers might interpret Jeff as having a midlife crisis. This would be wrong. Many men will act only when their pain and frustration is no longer manageable. A man who feels marginalized at midlife will either give in or run. Certainly, some men see this time as their last chance to "find themselves," and they embark on a self-destructive journey referred to as a midlife crisis. Nevertheless, not all men who leave their marriages in midlife do so to search for their own garden of personal happiness. Some do everything they can to make their relationships work but come up empty. These men feel driven from their homes by underappreciative wives. They feel contempt and criticism from the very women who claim to love them.

She Loves Me, She Loves Me Not

The mixed message of love *and* disdain create confusion for men. It's comparable to what a woman feels when a drunken husband or father beats or belittles her at night, only to show "love" in the morning. The emotional confusion is also intense for men who truly want to do what's right. They find their emotions moving up and down like a yo-yo on the end of a string. Add societal messages about irresponsible or stupid men to the mix, as well as wives who ridicule rather than encourage, and men have little reason to stay in a miserable marriage. It's little wonder that by the time they reach their forties or early fifties, some men decide to run. Like a dog that is kicked, a man either crawls away and licks his wounds or eventually bites back. Leaving a minimally functional relationship can be a man's way of preserving his emotional self and thus, his masculinity. This is not to say men should abandon difficult relationships, nor is it to suggest hardship is a precursor to failure. What I am saying is that a woman who fails to recognize her partner's need for respect and encouragement may be sowing the seeds of relational failure later on.

In today's society, many men do not fight back. They don't stand up for themselves. Where did we get the idea that turning the other cheek means a man has to become an emotional doormat? Others accept the idea that they're to die to their expectations for respect and intimacy, all under the guise of spiritual sainthood. They become like the dog who cowers under the table when scolded. Many of these men remain in their marriages, eventually becoming non-men, or, like Jeff, living parallel lives. The man in them dies. They give up. They eventually believe, and then develop, a distorted view of themselves. Perhaps they become cynical, jaded, angry, or passive. Whatever they do become, they lose a part of themselves in the process. Are these the kind of men that women want?

It doesn't take much to spot these beaten down men, some cudgeled into emotional compliance. The quid pro quo of a healthy, God-centered relationship is absent. These men don't smile. Like zombies, they don't move with enthusiasm or drive. They're dead men walking. They're the victims of a nefarious culture that treats men like moving targets in a cheap arcade. What becomes of the man who defends himself? The world sees him as a whiner, certainly not a real man because real men don't whine—they overcome.

What happens to men who refuse to defend themselves? The world sees them as henpecked weaklings who can't stand up for themselves. Do you see the dilemma? Most men remain silent victims who go about their daily lives living responsibly but receiving no credit for their effort. And men are becoming increasingly tired of this scenario.

The Midlife Conundrum: Taking Care of Business

Relationships are only one area in which men feel disconnected. Why do so many men wait until this time in their lives before doing something about their relationships? The answer is not so simple. The cumulative effects of a toxic relationship can begin to unravel at this stage when men reevaluate their lives. It may not be any single causal factor. It can be unresolved issues that collapse in on themselves, or that lead to an emotional affair like the one Jeff had. Whatever the case, many women don't understand what's happening. Unless they try to understand and act upon the needs of their mate, they will likely end up in a stale relationship or none at all. While women will say this is not what they want, most fail to recognize the symptoms leading to this reevaluation.

Midlife represents other unpleasant benchmarks for a man. It marks the waning of virility. It may be an unfulfilled dream or a receding hairline, but these realities peck away at the edge of a man's consciousness like vultures tearing the flesh off an animal carcass. If a man still has sons at home, he sees their masculinity budding while his is diminishing, another not-so-subtle reminder—he's losing his stamina and strength. Rather than embrace the mirror that once was his friend, he avoids it, afraid to see his own expansive waistline, graying hair, or wrinkled brow.

The way a man responds to his midlife doldrums reflects his character. His marriage and sex life may have become predictable if not altogether boring. He may run after other women, have an affair (emotional or physical), run a marathon, climb a mountain, or buy a Harley. If his marriage is stable and his wife empathetic, she will go through the journey with him. She will encourage him to seek challenge or change without compromising his faith or relationships in the process. By doing so, she shows empathy for her husband, and this empathy is not lost on him.

In much the same way a twelve- or thirteen-year-old boy tries to make his way into the world of men, a man in midlife tries to transition into the world of personal reality or truth. This reality is the way life is, rather than what he wishes it were. His reality may consist of unmet dreams and present truths about who he is and what he has become. It's a new transition, but it's no less frightening than the one he faced thirty or forty years before. It's the new emotional "Van Allen Belt" of his life, fraught with reentry risk and uncertainty. Most men navigate their reentry successfully; others do not. Those who don't make it will burn up or implode as they pass through this difficult and lonely place. At this point, men can no longer push aside the truth about who they are and what they want. Instead, a man must confront it just as he confronted other fears growing up. And he will confront the truths one more time—during his retirement years.

Humbled by Self-Truths

In the movie *City Slickers*, the character played by actor Billy Crystal asks his boss a question. "Have you ever reached a point in your life when you ask, 'Is this the best I'm ever gonna look? The best I'm ever going to feel, and it ain't that great?' " At midlife, Crystal synthesizes the way many men feel. His two urban companions are out to re-create adventure. Males don't just need adventure when they're growing up; they need it throughout life. Otherwise, they shrivel up and die, giving in to forces that make them feel more dead than alive. Most women don't grasp this need, but Crystal's wife does. She tells him to go out and find himself. Crystal has all but given up on adventure. He's worn-out. Men are like that today. They want more from life but lack fire in their bellies to go out and make it happen. Failure taunts them like a schoolyard bully, begging them to stand up and risk. As Crystal says to one of his friends, "At this age, you are where you are."

The negative self-truths can be devastating for men at midlife. Charles, now in his seventies, found himself caught in the aerospace layoffs of the mid-1960s. He never got back on track professionally. Since he had a family to care for, he began sweeping parking lots. With a degree in engineering and in his forties at the time, his self-esteem began to waver. More than thirty years later, he acts like a defeated man, grounded by the difficulties of life, stifled by what he accepted as true about himself. When he lost his job, Charles lost part of himself, and he never got it back. Work is important to most men. When they lose a job, for whatever reason, it can send them into a tailspin. A passive or sensitive man is vulnerable because he sees the loss of a job as a reflection of self, or at least he perceives it this way. He may view himself as worthless, powerless, vulnerable, or as a victim. The loss of a job can trigger strong emotions and lasting pain: anger, despair, depression, or other traditional midlife difficulties.

Self-Evaluation or Crisis?

Men like Jeff do not see themselves in a midlife crisis, at least not the way society defines it. Instead, they see their predicament as a culmination of countless miniature crises that lack resolution. "I reached a saturation point in my life," says Jeff. "It wasn't something I planned or ever expected. It didn't just happen overnight; it took years to boil to the surface because nothing important ever got resolved." Midlife is more a time of evaluation or introspection than a singular crisis. It can certainly lead to a crisis like the one Jeff faced, yet it would be a mistake to view every age-related change as a man's way of feeding a waning libido or escaping responsibility.

I see this stage more like a man who pulls over to the side of the highway of life to glance at a map. He asks himself, "Am I on the right road?" Of course, in the affairs of life and relationships, the right road often lacks the determinant nature of a map whose points are clear and unambiguous. Life is anything but clear for men in their late thirties through early fifties. Many who do pull to the side of the road find their maps blank and wonder why they were sold empty promises. Eventually they may conclude they did indeed get off at the correct exit in life, whereas other men continue to suffer from self-doubt. They begin to seek continuity to replace uncertainty. Instead of seeing this as self-deception, they should see it as a means of accepting the best truth a man can assemble about who he is.

A man in midlife has been humbled by experience, embarrassed by failure, wounded by rejection. Motivation withers, and his body grow soft. He wonders, "Did I get off at the wrong exit in life? Is this what I want? Is this all there will ever be?" He cloaks his mental anguish in clever and not-so-clever ways through sport, hobbies, or vice. If he conceals his pain, he remains pathologically unsound. A man must embrace his pain, understand his wounds, and accept his disappointment. Failure to do so will warp his definition of self. His masculinity will become twisted and obscure—tainted through self-deprecation and false perspective.

Am I Good Enough?

"I am a man at the margins. I am standing on the narrow strand between my failure and my aspirations, between what was and what will be, between my previous certainties and my present confusions, between my humanity and the Mystery."[1] Dr. Donald McCullough's description rings true for many men standing at their midlife crossroad. Many men are at the margins, and it's an uncomfortable place to be stuck. As McCullough reminds us, "Personal misery, whether small or large, always distorts perspective; no problem ever seems as large as your own."

At this stage of the game, a man wants a midlife checkup. He wants to know if he's "making it." He wants to know if he's "good enough." The same question reveals itself in many ways. "What am I good at doing?" "Am I a good person, father, or husband?" By midlife, a man has had enough time and experience to answer part of these important questions. He may point to things he has accomplished. He may look at selfless acts to bless his wife, children, or community. If he's married, he may seek his answer from his wife, though this can be problematic and risky. Negative reinforcement at this stage can push a man into depression or ignite a genuine crisis. Sensitivity, empathy, and encouragement are the gifts a woman can confer on her husband. If he receives a stifling barrage that reminds him of his own inadequacies or ways he has not measured up, he will wither, leave, or both.

A man's overriding question is not about physical attributes or educational attainment, though these are important to him. It's deeper than that. It's about looking into his soul and prying out the goodness. He's seeking affirmation. A positive evaluation in midlife is often sufficient to carry a man through to his golden years. If he genuinely feels he's on the right path, has made the right decisions and learned to give of himself to others, he will find his way to contentment. This is rarely an easy transition. Because it's difficult, many men suppress it, pushing it into their subconscious, or delaying it indefinitely. As a result, these men cheat themselves.

If you think affirmation isn't important, look at the life of Christ. At an immensely critical time in the beginning of his ministry (baptism), God said, "You are my Son, whom I love; with you I am well pleased" (Luke 3:22). Notice the three profound things God said to his Son.

1. *You are my Son.* A reminder of belonging. Every man and every son has a place. He needs to be reminded of who he is and where he's from.
2. *Whom I love.* A reminder of his value. Every man and every son needs to know he's valued and embraced.
3. *With you I am well pleased.* A reminder that he is worthy. Every man and every son needs affirmation.

These words spoken by God to his very own Son were spoken at the right time. They set the course of Christ's ministry. They would get Jesus through the toughest of times—even death. Every earthly father should speak the same words, or similar ones, to his son. They also will get his son through tough times, tribulations, trials, and pain. One other point to note. The Father did not speak these words to Jesus in secret; he spoke them openly and unashamedly.

God also spoke prophetically about the coming Messiah: "Here is my servant, whom I uphold, my chosen one in whom I delight" (Isa. 42:1). Now let me ask you a question. If the Son of God felt the love and acceptance of the Father, why do men require less? It doesn't make a man needy or insecure to want to know if he's good enough, if he's worthy, if he's loved.

It's a yearning in the heart of men to hear, "Well done." Sad and pathetic, men beg for it. They grovel for crumbs of attention. Healthy men truly appreciate it. A woman can affirm the man closest to her. She can speak positive life-giving truth to the man she cares about. This man doesn't cease to be a healthy man when the woman he loves shares verbal kindness. A sick or unhealthy woman sees affirming a man as a way of de-affirming herself. She withholds verbal, emotional, or physical approval as punishment. Other women may lack the capacity for forgiveness or empathy. They hold out on their men because their men have held out on them. This is a vicious cycle of emotional toxicity. The bottom line is that a man needs other men, and certainly his own wife, to affirm him for what he does right.

Richard is a fifty-one-year-old divorced man with three children. With a master's degree in finance, he works in international banking. By all accounts, he's successful. He pays more than his share to help his children attend private school and goes out of his way to bless them. Still, like many men his age, he needed to develop a clear picture of who he is as a man. "I came to grips with the fact that I may never be materially successful. What I do have is my knowledge and experiences." For Richard, evaluating where he is in life after five decades of living includes self-truths and self-reflection that encompasses more than money or possessions. While many American men fixate on the material, others, like Richard, point to different markers—family, education, experience, service, personal happiness, or spiritual growth. Whatever benchmarks a man uses to evaluate his midlife success or failure, these become his unique way of validating himself and accepting his place in life.

Accepting Physical Challenges and Change

It doesn't take a genius at fifty to recognize physical changes. In my previous book, *Staying Fit After 40,* I talk about some of the specific changes that occur after a man turns forty. These include stiff muscles and longer recovery time after tough workouts. Muscle tone diminishes, our ability to process oxygen efficiently declines, and recovery from minor or major injuries requires more time. These physical changes can lead to injuries for middle-aged men who think they can play just as hard as they did in their twenties. The fast running with quick lateral movements send men to the emergency room with broken knees, separated shoulders, or torn tendons. It isn't worth it. A man wants to believe he can still perform at the same level he did twenty years ago, but some men must learn the hard way—they cannot.

The good news is that the physically active man can offset the effects of aging. The same man at forty or fifty can be *functionally* fitter than men in their thirties. A healthy lifestyle makes the difference. This means no smoking or excessive use of alcohol, reducing stress, staying active, and eating well. The core healthy ingredients are regular exercise, good eating habits (both content and consumption), and adequate sleep. A man who practices these three life-extending habits also helps reduce long-term stress—a precursor to malfunctions in the immune system and susceptibility to certain kinds of cancer.

At midlife, a man must also come to grips with his physical abilities and appearance. As testosterone levels decline, libido goes with it. Wrinkles, hair loss, decreased muscle tone, and extra weight around the middle are common maladies. These and other markers, such as watching parents grow old, leads to mortality thinking. It isn't that a man has a morbid obsession with death. Rather, he recognizes time is running out—his time. Many men begin to reflect. They think about their own father and may gain a new appreciation for his contributions and sacrifice. A man at midlife begins to identify with his father, though this rarely occurs until he has been through his own life struggles, family strain, loss, or introspection.

As thoughts of mortality arise, a man may find himself taking furtive glances at the obituary column. There he sees other men, perhaps his age or younger, succumbing to illness. It sparks the internal question about whether he's living as well as he could be. John is a good example. He's a forty-nine-year-old middle-school teacher, trying to assess his own life and choices. "I began thinking that I have about twenty to twenty-five active summers left," says John. "I started to tick off all the things I want to accomplish in my life and realized I better get with it!" For many of us, life passes more quickly than we ever imagined. We rarely think about opportunities until it's too late.

By midlife, men feel time is slipping away from them and may suddenly try to make up for lost years or the years spent raising their kids. No man can cram twenty years of adventure into one or two; it just doesn't work. Those who try, end up wearing out their bank accounts, bodies, or relationships. A wiser choice is to reassess our lives and establish new goals. This means creating a self-accountability system to keep us on the right track for the years ahead.

Love, Sex, and Stable Relationships

Steve and Bob recently turned fifty. Both attend church and place high value on meaningful relationships. Each was married more than twenty-five years, until recently. They have children, solid reputations in the community, and are genuinely nice guys. So what happened to their marriages? Neither wanted a divorce, and both worked hard in counseling to avoid it. Steve's wife smothered and mothered him while refusing physical intimacy. She flatly refused to engage in any outdoor activities that were important to Steve. She said she wanted the marriage to last but did almost nothing to preserve it.

In Bob's case, his wife found another man. She refused counseling and launched into her own midlife crisis. I watched it happen. I met with Bob, encouraged him, and prayed for him. At the time I said, "Bob, she will soon regret what she's done; you're a good man." And he is—tender, gentle, well liked. It wasn't enough. Neither Bob nor Steve nor Jeff has remarried, though Bob's wife is starting to have second thoughts about the greener-grass syndrome. Now here's the interesting part. Each of these men still cares about his ex-wife. There is no sense of anger. In each case, reconciliation was (and may still be) possible. It's God's desire to restore and renew tattered relationships. Yet this never occurs within a vacuum. Nor can it occur when one party, man or woman, clings to old ways of relating that didn't work. A willingness to change is always the first step in healing. A willingness to *make* the change is the next step. Recognizing problems is not enough, but it's a start.

The reassessment that goes on inside midlife men involves their basic need for intimacy. If men are in a stale or unsupportive relationship, they feel the loss more deeply. While sex is still important, it becomes less urgent in the forties and fifties. Theoretically, he becomes a better lover. He's patient, less egocentric, and more in tune with giving pleasure rather than only receiving it. Sex in midlife can be better than when he was in his twenties and thirties. Of course, this is not true for all men. Some men seek proof of their virility and power to attract women—especially younger women. King David, at about the age of forty, did so with Bathsheba; the consequences were tragic.

If a man feels he's little more than a broken appendage in his marriage, he will look for intimacy elsewhere. There are reasons that men or women have affairs. While Christian tradition and most churches excoriate men for giving in to their impulses, few address the underlying reasons men are vulnerable in the first place. I wonder if the church doesn't do a disservice to men by blaming them for giving in to the very desires their Creator put within them? This is not an excuse for men to behave badly. Rather, it's an indictment of a lopsided system of blame. In his book, *Love and Respect*, Dr. Emerson Eggerichs says, "The cold, hard truth is that men are often lured into affairs because they are sexually deprived at home. A man who strays is usually given total blame for his affair, but in many cases he is a victim of temptation that his wife helped bring upon him."[2]

For years, Christian men have been told that sex begins in the kitchen. The truth is, men today change more diapers, do more laundry, wash more dishes, and make more meals than in any previous generation. While some men may do these chores to get sex in return, the majority do so because they want to be helpful. Are they getting more physical intimacy because they help? In most instances, the answer is clearly no. Ron, a marketing professional in his forties, explains his own dilemma. "I spent years working on the cars, gathering wood, cleaning dishes, washing laundry, vacuuming, painting, and just about anything you can imagine. My wife didn't care. It was never enough. I began to feel like an unpaid domestic laborer!"

If sex begins in the kitchen, neither Jeff nor Steve experienced it. But for midlife men, it isn't only about sex; it's also about kindness, affirmation, recognition, and respect. Men are hammered by the media and guilt-laden by the church. They want more from their spouses than scorn. They want their wives to see them as more than domestic help. This is what women have wanted too, and rightly so. Women don't like to be treated as a sex object or housekeeper. Yet when women use sex as a weapon, consciously or unconsciously, they eventually get hurt. It's a dead-end street. Men rebel because they need more from the women who say they love them. This is not to say men are always sensitive to the women in their lives. Clearly, some are not. And I recognize women need emotional intimacy, but a woman who ignores a man's need for sex is sowing the seeds for her own hurt, and possibly even the demise of her marriage.

Bill is a professional in his forties. His frustration is with another problem few men talk about but many feel. In speaking candidly about his wife of twenty-plus years, he says, "She mothers me, and I'm sick of it." Most men do not want to be mothered. At midlife a man needs space to pursue new activities. If his wife is not growing in her own sense of independence, she will revert to what she knows best—mothering. Healthy men don't want this. The men who are attracted to women who mother are attracted for reasons other than romance. If she has children moving out of the home, she will redouble her efforts, and a healthy man will retreat. Men want mothering about as much as they look forward to a prostate exam! "Any time I leave the home, my wife asks who I had seen, what I did, or what my conversations were about," Bill explains. "I feel smothered. I feel distrusted. Every time I am a few minutes late, I feel I owe her some big explanation, as if I have been a naughty boy." There is a fine line between mutual accountability and feeling smothered. A healthy, God-centered relationship allows room for both individual and joint growth. To the extent that a woman lives vicariously through her husband or children, she will find her own midlife transition even more difficult.

Finding Our Way Home

In her book, *Understanding Men's Passages*, author Gail Sheehy says, "The greatest harmony in marriage comes from seeking and finding a creative resolution to a major life passage, together."[3] Men want solid, loving relationships today more than ever. They need them. That so many men are searching for "the one" is evidence they're not finding their "soul mate." Men want a place to belong. They want a place they feel safe. They want women who champion them, encourage them, and reach out to them.

For most men, the road map home is unclear. They face challenges in the workplace, in their marriages, with their kids, and even with their bodies. It's a tough time. To keep their relationships vibrant, men must navigate successfully around mines hidden beneath the surface of their emotional lives. As I mentioned, a sensitive and empathetic wife tries to understand these pressures and does what she can to mollify them. An unfeeling wife will exacerbate the pain a man feels and may inadvertently set off one or more of the mines if she is not in tune with his needs.

Every man comes through his midlife assessment differently. If he's wise, he will weigh the consequences to major decisions. If he allows his emotional fragility, insecurity, or disappointment to prevail, he will likely give up far more than he ever hopes or believes he can gain. Ideally, he will harness both the intellectual and spiritual wisdom that comes from burgeoning maturity and sound judgment. For men stuck in their own midlife crunch-time, keeping the following principles in mind will help ease the transition.

1. *Stay accountable to other men.* Men find strength and solace in the presence of other men who have been through their own struggles.
2. *Stay connected to what matters most—church, friends, children, spouse.*
3. *Venture out in healthy ways.* If you plan to try something new, don't jeopardize your faith, your family, or your values.
4. *Reevaluate with caution.* It's easy to see your glass as half empty at midlife. The reassessment time should include more inner work (soul work) and introspection.
5. *Make major decisions slowly.* Beware of making drastic, life-altering changes without consultation, prayer, and fore-thought.
6. *Reject typically false notions that the grass is greener on the other side.*
7. *Recognize that you are in a phase.* Whatever hardship, angst, or turmoil you find yourself in will eventually pass.
8. *Embrace the test.* God may seem silent, but he will not abandon you at your point of greatest need. As Job said, "Though he slay me, yet will I hope in him" (Job 13:15).
9. *Protect your health.* Take care of your physical and emotional life. Be active, engage in new learning experiences, manage stress, and avoid substance abuse.

10. *Establish new goals.* It's easy to be stuck in a rut. Ruts are comfortable because they're familiar. Break out and try something new—education, hobbies, travel, or volunteering.

In his insightful book, *The Long Journey Home*, Os Guinness states what should be obvious to all. He says there are "three essentials for a fulfilling life: a clear sense of personal identity, a strong sense of purpose and mission, and a deep sense of faith and meaning."[4]

CHAPTER 7

The Golden Boys
Is That All There Is?

THERE WAS little that fazed him. A pillar of strength, his mind and ideas were a step ahead of others. He enjoyed respect from his peers, had the boundless energy of a teenager, and the drive of an inventor. His zest for life, work, and ministry kept him running at a high-octane pace. Now he's an octogenarian, and we talk about his life.

His mood is dark, not from regretful choices but from loss itself—or, rather, from the loss *of* self. Robert's light blue eyes are glassy. His hands are weathered and worn; old scars from a lifetime show against his tan skin. He walks slowly, carefully, grabbing the nearest railing for support—just in case. His mind is active, but deep sadness and disappointment form an unmistakable mask across his weathered face.

Married more than fifty years, his grown children love and honor him and his seventeen grandchildren admire him. He survived the depression years, the Great War, succeeded in business, met prime ministers and presidents, and had a positive impact on thousands of people through his life and ministry. Today, however, Robert suffers from depression. Though he has been a Christian since his midthirties, he can't find a way out of his emotional swamp. He's a good man who lived a good life and honored God. He will leave a legacy that will last generations. So what's the problem?

Millions of men in the twilight of their lives, much like Robert, cannot find peace. Just beneath the surface of their emotional lives is a nagging sense of discontentment. There is no single defining answer to this emotional malaise. It engulfs scores of men in their so-called Golden Years, a less-than-adequate description for the postretirement years. So what exactly do they feel? They feel marginalized by society and put out to pasture at work. At home, they're in the way; in stores, they're invisible to young salesclerks. In talking with Robert and other older men, I find several telltale clues to their sense of lostness. For some men, it manifests itself as a deep sense of sadness. Perhaps it shouldn't, but it does.

In general, men at the end of their lives are reflective, pensive, humble, and mature. Cecil, now in his seventies, is a writer, as well as a former pastor and missionary. He says, "Being who I am and enjoying my life are my focus. For most of my life, I felt as if my role was to please God and care for others. Those things weren't wrong, but I got lost somewhere in the march of time. I had no idea what I wanted for myself." There is that word again—*lost*. As most people who are long past the midlife marker will tell you, time seems to accelerate as we get older. Perhaps it has something to do with our growing collection of experiences or the feeling we have not measured up to our own expectations, and there is no time left to change our predicament.

There is an unmistakable changing of the guard between the parents of Baby Boomers (the World War II generation) and Baby Boomers themselves (born between 1946 and 1962). The greatest transfer of wealth in history, estimated to be well more than $1 trillion, is already under way. While Boomers fought to find themselves, their fathers held it together during the storms of life. They were tough, stoic, trustworthy, and consistent, and they tried, with some success, to pass along these same values to their sons. This generation of men and women, who are now in their later years, embody clear and unmistakable values. It's little wonder the postmodern world seems as foreign to them as the beaches of Normandy. The World War II generation believed in values larger than self, and they were willing to sacrifice for what they believed. Here is a quick review of some of these values.

1. They bought the American dream and didn't look back, amassing more wealth than any generation that came before them.
2. They believe and practice honor and commitment. A handshake could cement a business deal; a poorly functioning marriage might remain intact because commitment is more important than personal freedom.
3. They're intolerant of dishonor (family, nation, and friends).
4. They disdain disloyalty, believing that loyalty is virtuous.
5. They believe sacrifice is an accepted part of life.
6. They believe work is a privilege and laziness is weakness.
7. They worked for honor, upward mobility, and commitment to family, not just to find personal fulfillment.
8. They amassed wealth and assets but refused to cling to them selfishly.
9. They're generous, giving to philanthropic causes for the betterment of those in need, not because giving fills a latent need within themselves.
10. They're humble and grateful, recognizing where they came from.
11. They have a robust social network that often lasts a lifetime.
12. They're frugal, recognizing that material success is difficult to achieve but easy to lose.

Though certainly not exhaustive or flawless, this list of generational traits is a snapshot into why men from this generation think the way they do. They see the world differently than their Boomer sons because their worldview is not the same. In a few short generations, dramatic and rapid-fire change sent shockwaves through these men accustomed to stability. It's no wonder these men in today's Golden Years look on in perplexity, confusion, or disillusionment. The world is not the morally predictable place it once was.

For most men, the midlife years are like an emotional checkup. They wonder, "How am I doing?" By the time a man reaches the Golden Years, he's asking the same question but in an entirely different way. He asks, "How did I do?" For the most part, he looks backward, rather than forward. Where else is there to go? By now, either he has accomplished the big things of life or he hasn't. He has developed a record of accomplishment that speaks well of himself, or he has been a failure. If he concludes the latter, and many men do, his psychological state of mind suffers. Even good men have regrets. Men like Robert wonder if they did enough, did it well, or could have prioritized better. It's too late to rewrite the script, and by now they know it.

Did I Make a Difference?

The older man, perhaps in his late seventies, walks silently through the cemetery in France. His face is that of a man who has seen a ghost or watched some awful accident. Etched in the subconscious is a nagging question, and he has come to find the answer. An American flag darts back and forth to the unsteady rhythm of the unseen wind. In the background is the expansive blue of the Atlantic and the beaches below. In the cemetery, the camera pans countless rows of white crosses and an occasional star of David. This is Normandy. This is where it all happened.

The man walks ahead of his family, who has joined him in his search. A son, granddaughters, a wife—they trail behind, sensing the solemn moment. He's alone with his memories and pain. He searches for names on the crosses until he finds one he recognizes. A tear forms in his eye as he remembers events from a distant past. In the movie *Saving Private Ryan*, the older man kneels at the grave site of the character played by Tom Hanks. The older Ryan speaks aloud, as if his dead sergeant can hear him. "Every day I think about what you said to me that day on the bridge. I have tried to live the best that I could. I hope it was enough, that in your eyes I have earned what all of you have done for me."

The old man stands upright, remembering the words a dying sergeant whispered into his ear fifty years prior: "Earn this; earn it." Now Ryan stands, decades later, wondering if he made a big enough difference with his life. In his own way, every man asks the same question. But the scene is not over yet. Private Ryan turns to his wife and says, "Tell me I have lived a good life. Tell me I'm a good man." Notice that he doesn't ask it as a question; he's afraid of the answer, as all men are. His wife *understands* his pain and answers with two words: "You are." At the end, that's enough.

Ralph Waldo Emerson summed up success this way: "To laugh often and much; to win the respect of intelligent people and the affection of children; to earn the appreciation of honest critics and endure the betrayal of false friends; to appreciate beauty, to find the best in others; to leave the world a little better, whether by a healthy child, a garden patch or a redeemed social condition; to know even one life has breathed easier because you have lived. This is the meaning of success."[1] While Emerson is right about so much, he misses the central issue. Christ said, "What good will it be for a man if he gains the whole world, yet forfeits his soul?" (Matt. 16:26). Ultimately, it all comes down to that one final question.

Older men want to know they made a difference, that what they did with their lives mattered. In the movie *About Schmidt*, the opening scene pans the gray skies and dreary landscape near Omaha, Nebraska. Warren, the character played by Jack Nicholson, is retiring from his job. It's his last day. He sits among empty boxes in a stark office, his eyes glued to the clock above the door, waiting for the second hand to strike the top of the hour. When it does, he stands, puts on his coat, and takes a last glance around. Later that evening, Warren sits passively at his retirement dinner. The platitudes are meaningless. There is something far deeper going on inside of him. He seems to be thinking, "What am I to do next?" "What happens tomorrow?" He's supposed to be happy, to recognize he has achieved some grand milestone. But Warren is not happy. Eventually he wanders over to the bar and sits alone.

Before vacating the party in his honor, however, Warren listens to his closest friend give a retirement speech. He looks at Warren and says, "How do you feel about these young punks taking over our jobs? It seems like some kind of conspiracy to me. I know something about retirement . . . all these gifts don't mean a thing. What means something is to know you've devoted your life to something meaningful, being productive, to raising a fine family, to building a fine house, to be respected by your community, to having wonderful lasting friendships; at the end of his career, to look back and enjoy riches far beyond the monetary kind."

It sounds good and right, but still something is missing. So what is it? It's *meaning*. It is *purpose*. It's *legacy*. It's a realization that even Robert, a Christian who devoted much of his life to ministry, feels it.

Weighed in the Balance and Found Wanting

Some men live as if tomorrow will never come. Others live as if it's already here. The former live in fear and denial, while the latter walk a melancholic line toward the gallows. One day they awaken (if they ever do) to find their lives have been wasted. The king of Babylon is a classic example. He thought life was about parties, sex, and drinking, which is how he spent much of his time. The king and his friends thought the good times would roll on forever. They didn't. In fact, this particular story tells of the last big party King Belshazzar would ever have.

God spoke to the king in an unusual way, through handwriting on the wall of the banquet room. The king was a weak-kneed man in a literal sense. Once he saw the handwriting, "his face turned pale and he was so frightened that his knees knocked together and his legs gave way" (Dan. 5:6). The heavenly language was unreadable, so the king had to find an interpreter. Well, actually, it was the queen's idea. Although she was not partying with the other guests, she did know about Daniel's reputation. And there is something to be said about our reputation following us wherever we go; fortunately, for Daniel, what was said about him was good. "There is a man in your kingdom who has the spirit of the holy gods in him," said the queen (v. 11). That was his reputation. And then the Bible tells us, "This man Daniel . . . was found to have a keen mind and knowledge and understanding, and also the ability to interpret dreams, explain riddles and solve difficult problems" (v. 12). He sounds like the kind of man we could use in our world today.

Once he arrived on the scene, Daniel's character immediately became clear. He refused the gifts and promotion—to number three man in the kingdom—that the king offered. Nor did Daniel mince words before the number one man, the king himself. In fact, he accused him of ignorance, arrogance, rebellion against God, theft, and blasphemy (see vv. 22, 23). Daniel said, "But you did not honor the God who holds in his hand your life and all your ways" (v. 23). We forget, young or old, that our lives are in God's hands, and each day is a gift from him. We forget the fragility of life, the blessing of his providence, the truth that we will one day have to give an account to him.

Daniel's interpretation of the writing on the wall was stunning. In brief, he said to the king, "God has numbered the days of your reign and brought it to an end. You have been weighed on the scales and found wanting" (vv. 26, 27). No man wants to hear these damning words. They're an indictment. Just a few hours before, the king was celebrating and enjoying life. He had no idea how soon he would have to give an accounting for his life. Do any of us have a clue when that time will come for us?

The Bible is replete with examples of men who failed to consider the end. I think of Herod, who listened to John the Baptist preach but never made any change in his immoral lifestyle. The Bible tells us Herod "liked to listen to him" (Mark 6:20). Then there is the parable of the rich fool. He thought his life was about accumulating wealth. "But God said to him, 'You fool! This very night your life will be demanded from you' " (Luke 12:20).

Is twenty-first-century America any different from ancient Babylon? I don't think so. No man thinks tonight is his night. He wants to believe he still has time—perhaps not a lot of time, but time nonetheless. As men, we vacillate between a false sense of invincibility and a nagging understanding that our days are numbered. We're walking contradictions. Yet we inevitably reach a point where we question our legacy, those tidbits of our character that have fallen like pixie dust on those around us.

Lives of Quiet Desperation

My uncle, Dr. Duane Walker, is a healthy, intelligent, and enormously successful man of seventy-eight who also ponders his own legacy. After retiring from his pastorate (a church of 1,400 members), he quotes from Henry David Thoreau: "Most people live lives of quiet desperation." He says, "I ponder the question of legacy, and when I do I am often left with the feeling of disappointment or of having fallen short." Fallen short? These words intrigue and befuddle me. Duane used his own determinedness and hard work to find his way in the world. Here's how he did it.

> In putting myself through college, I carried hod [wet cement] during the summers for a Los Angeles masonry contractor; putting myself through seminary, I worked an all-night shift at the Oakland YMCA and weekends at Trader Vic's Restaurant in San Francisco, returning to my Berkeley room at 2:00 or 3:00 a.m. In Boston I worked at an orphanage as a youth director in a Congregational church, riding the streetcars for transportation in snowy winters, living in a third-floor flat with a bathtub in the kitchen, and working on language requirements of French, German, and Greek, in addition to writing a doctoral dissertation. The work ethic has always characterized my modus operandi, an ethic I inherited from my parents. There was not a lazy bone in the family or any sense of "entitlement."

Talk to many parents today, and they will tell you a different story. Their kids don't want to take a low-paying job in a fast-food restaurant or bus tables until well past midnight. They would never ride public transportation. The idea of sacrifice is lost. Today, "sacrifice" means not having the best cell plan (with thousands of optional downloadable ring tones), a late model car, or designer clothes. This present generation is drowning in rights. Former Supreme Court nominee Robert Bork calls this "radical individualism." In a world that moves at lightning speed, there is precious little time to waste. If it isn't fun, doesn't feel good, takes too much work, time, or money, why do it? "Sensations must be steadily intensified if boredom is to be kept at bay," wrote Bork. "A culture obsessed with technology will come to value personal convenience above almost all else, and ours does."[2] This entitlement attitude, however, is both foreign and confusing to the Golden Boys.

Jack MacDonald, a seventy-five-year-old former congressional representative from Montana, said he learned to work early and to work hard. "The war was on. All the men were gone, so every kid had a job. We had seven teams of horses, and I started driving a team when I was ten. We kept the milk cool by putting it in a spring-fed creek that ran between the house and the barn. We didn't have electricity until I was in college." MacDonald's own son, Kelly, learned from his father. One day he went to the golf course in Kalispell and told the manager, "I will work for free for two days to show you what I can do." He was hired the following day. Kelly now tells his dad, "Thanks for the legacy and for teaching me how to work." Today, the elder MacDonald's advice is to "always do a good job, and always finish a job, even if you lose money."

This is clearly not the kind of advice most young men receive today. "Work for nothing? Are you crazy?" The reason this concept is unfamiliar to recent generations is that it's not just about money; it's about character. Strong character involves choices and principles that are bigger than the individual. When self rules supreme, character becomes the victim of expedience.

Breeding Grounds of
Anxiety and Obsolescence

The thought of death, ill health, or legacy occupy our conscious or unconscious minds, like vultures waiting to pounce on our troubled souls. The big three do not act alone to peck away at our sense of self. Clearly, material success plays a role in how men view themselves, even in their Golden Years. A padded bank account might make life more comfortable, but it does not answer the pressing question of *worthiness*, the kind Robert still finds elusive.

There is another uncomfortable consequence of the culture-shift. It's change. For men in their Golden Years, facing unprecedented change is, well, discomfiting to say the least. It's particularly hard because these men have always been in control. Now, they're losing control. That this would add to their already weakened sense of self comes as little surprise. While change has always been an inevitable part of life, something is different about the warp speed at which change is now occurring. The prophet Daniel wrote about the end times, "Many will go here and there to increase knowledge" (Dan. 12:4). In a world that places high value on information, we have lost the ability to *understand* much of that information. One by-product is the overabundance of choices. Another is the difficulty in keeping pace with a rapidly changing world.

Information-overload leads to information-anxiety in four main ways, according to Nathan Shedroff. Information-anxiety is:

1. The frustration we feel with our inability to keep up with the amount of data present in our lives.
2. A frustration with the quality of what we encounter—especially what passes as news.
3. The guilt we feel for not being better informed, of not keeping up with the amount of data masquerading as information.
4. The dangerous hubris that develops for "knowing things first."[3]

We rarely ask ourselves the truly important questions, let alone search for the answers. First, what do we need to know, and why do we need to know it? Second, what are the costs associated with what we know? We're told that knowledge is power, but power for what? Simply knowing doesn't make us wise or powerful. Discernment is what is missing.

As previously mentioned, the idea that more is better when it comes to choices represents the twisted values of a materialistic, market-driven society. How many choices do we need to be content? Our super product-saturated society is drowning in "stuff" but devoid of what really matters—vibrant relationships. Take a glance in your garage or closet and ask yourself if you're an exception to this more-is-better mentality. We suffer from the confusion of surplus, and it leads to the false belief that worthiness, security, and happiness are based on having things we don't really need. Effective marketing is supposed to make us feel dissatisfied with what we have, not the other way around. The more we subject ourselves to marketing messages, the less satisfaction we feel. So, one wonders, why do we fall for this nonsense? It's simple: it makes us *feel* better. Remember the bumper sticker, "The one who dies with the most toys, wins"? When we permit our self-esteem or masculinity to be contingent on amassing stuff, we miss the important questions that nag at our soul.

Rapid change increases uncertainty; uncertainty intensifies anxiety; anxiety breeds fear—and fear can lead to depression. Depression is a way of giving up, of throwing in the towel, and a great many Golden Boys fall into that trap as they see themselves as rusting hulks in the scrapyard. They aren't. This generation has so much to pass along, but newer generations are just not listening, let alone asking the right questions. If there is a remedy for men like Robert, it's to reengage. As we will see in a moment, the adventure of youth need not be lost as a man moves into his Golden Years; in fact, learning can offset the malady of obsolescence.

Transitioning Well

Jim is sixtysomething, fit, and retired . . . sort of. When I first saw him around town, he was riding his bike between jobs tuning pianos. Jim and I began playing squash together, and I soon discovered he was a smart player. Squash is like a physical game of chess, and Jim always seemed to hit the hard black ball where I wasn't. When we finished playing, we talked about politics, religion, and volunteer work. This relationship went on for more than a year, and more than once, I thought to myself, "This guy is pretty smart for a piano tuner!" Jim failed to mention one small detail about his life: he holds a doctoral degree in political science. Jim had been a professor at Texas A&M, but few knew about it—including me. And that's just part of the story.

When Jim moved to our small town in north Idaho, he did odd jobs—a Christmas tree trimmer, a garbage collector, and construction helper. These are hardly the kind of jobs I equate with a university professor. Jim and I talked about the Golden Years, as well as his life and experiences. I asked him about his latest adventure—a 154-mile solo kayaking trip through the Florida Keys. He has also kayaked the Hudson and Columbia rivers. He's hitchhiked across Europe and parts of Latin America. His volunteer work includes private schools, Habitat for Humanity, TV Turnoff Week, and church work. His formula for success is balance—physical activities, intellectual stimulation, adventure, social investments, volunteer work, and involvement with his church.

Jim said to me, "What is life? What is living? It's not just keeping the heart beating. It's about putting all of our God-given capabilities to work." As technology and new inventions make our lives easier, do they really make them better? As Jim observes from experience, "The hard way is almost always the most rewarding." In modern culture, we want simple solutions and easy answers, though these rarely yield the kind of valuable lessons that help us grow. Even our physical limitations in postretirement serve as a nagging reminder there is no cure-all for what ails us. "You always have the challenge of using what you have left," says Jim. "It's a feeling of achievement to accomplish something without being whole. You need to learn to do the best with what you've got. When you do that, you're happiest."

As strength fades and stamina wanes, it's tempting for some men to throw in the towel. Some give in to the pleas of a worrisome spouse, aches, pains, or the remote control. It's always easier to give up or to give in, but that isn't God's way and it isn't his plan. Retirement-aged men must fight to keep the adventure alive. They must battle for meaningfulness lest they collapse into the abyss of despair. Just as it was in childhood, the place to find the needed adventure is rarely with the woman, the mother, the wife. It's in a deeper place. As my friend Jim was preparing for his trip to the Florida Keys, another friend's wife said, "You can't do that; you might get killed!" But isn't that the point? This same need for a woman to nurture and to feel secure, which she once used to protect her children, now keeps men in their recliners during the Golden Years. It shouldn't— and it mustn't. The husband of the woman who expressed such concern over Jim's pending trip to the Keys told Jim, "I feel like a prisoner on my own couch." When he wants to go hunting, his wife tells him, "You might get hurt. You might get killed. It's dangerous." Yes, it's dangerous, and that's exactly why men need the adventure, whether they're twenty or thirty, six or sixty.

There is a great line in the *Sound of Music*, words spoken by Captain Von Trapp to his fiancée before he dumped her for Maria. He said, "Activity suggests a life filled with purpose." The assumption, of course, is that it does not. While adventure and activity are important, the need to remain active for the sake of activity alone leaves us feeling hollow. This is especially true, if, as so many golden-aged men have come to believe, their sense of self or masculinity is tied to productivity alone.

Older men must resist the urge for the easy way out—the artificial adventure. It never satisfies the longing of a man's soul. No, the adventure is always personal. As Eldredge puts it in *Wild at Heart*, "So many guys have been told to put that adventurous spirit behind them, and 'be responsible,' meaning only live for duty."[4] The adventure may change, but it must never stop—God wired men this way. Your body will rebel, your mind will falter, and your energy will diminish. So what? As Jim says, "Will you use these as excuses, or will you push on?"

Because men find so much of their worth in what they do, they must keep the variable controls of adventure alive. It won't be easy. Just trying to navigate the in-box of their cell phone, program a remote control, or learn new software can be daunting. Weak limbs, thin skin, or poorly lubricated joints serve as a reminder they can no longer storm the beaches of Normandy. Nonetheless, there is no rule that says a man must give up at sixty-five or seventy-five and start traveling the country in a motor home. This is not to say men shouldn't accept their physical limits and revise their expectations. No one wants to watch an aging ballplayer try to squeeze another year or two from his waning career. We want our heroes to finish on the top of their game and make effective transitions that include mentoring the next generation. Moses did it. David did it. Jesus did it. We can do it too.

Men in their postretirement years must not let others—a spouse, children, wealth, past mistakes, or society—define their worthiness. To the extent that older men accept their obsolescence, they will become so. Every man lives with some regret—a lost opportunity, a broken relationship, or a road not taken. While reflection is valuable, it should be used to make amends wherever possible, not to slip into despair. It's important that we focus as much or more on what we did right, the people whose lives we touched in a positive way, the accomplishments, and the selfless acts.

The Golden Years are not the end; they're the precursor to the end. Time and relationships are most important. Broken relations are redeemable. Invest yourself in people. Use your time strategically. Invest your energy effectively.

Here are ten specific words of advice from men in their Golden Years:

1. *Slow down.* Cec Murphey is the author or coauthor of more than one hundred books. He says, "I have slowed down my life somewhat. Everything doesn't have to be completed

within the next twenty minutes. I'm more patient with people. I've learned to value my health, my family, my lifestyle." In the prime of our lives, men feel the need to be productive—to engage in their purpose. By the time most men reach the twilight of their lives, they no longer need to compete, produce, or perform at the same levels. As Murphey says, "The purpose of life isn't to be productive."

2. *Stay physically active.* The body is tired, the muscles are weak, and the vigor of previous years is gone—forever. God made men to work. Even in retirement, men need to stay active to maintain muscle tone, strength, and endurance. Join a health club or a walking group, or buy exercise equipment. Make exercise a part of your daily routine. By doing so, you help offset the effects of osteoporosis, heart disease, diabetes, and various forms of cancer.

3. *Focus on the family.* Allen, now in his early sixties, encourages men to invest more in family. In the end, what matters most are people, not things. People should matter to us because they matter to God. The same is true for family. The investment we make in people will determine our legacy.

4. *Reach out socially.* As seventy-eight-year-old Duane Walker says, "Focus on relationships and inner-wholeness." He suggests men find healing and support through a few close friends—not scores of friends, just a handful who know you for what and who you are. Isolation can lead to depression, so avoid falling into this trap.

5. *Revise your expectations.* Sixty-four-year-old former pastor Eddie Smith says, "Men look to their job to communicate their masculinity." Men don't need to do this anymore. Instead, they need to reorient their thinking and redirect their efforts to passing on expertise by mentoring or teaching.

6. *Volunteer.* Give back. A salesperson his entire life, once he retired, eighty-three-year-old Al started holding and rock-

ing newborn babies at a nearby hospital. Other men choose to serve on boards, as chaplains in the jails, assist widows or single women with repair work, volunteer at local libraries or schools, or help at their churches.

7. *Stay intellectually engaged.* Dr. Walker says, "I have had an intellectual curiosity that keeps me busy. Seldom, almost never, am I without at least a couple of books on the burner." Reading, thinking, meditating, discussing, learning—these are ways to stay engaged.

8. *Make a plan.* Organize how you will invest your time and energy. Make a list of things you want to do in a day, or week. Write them down and check them off as you accomplish them. Write a letter, run an errand, call a friend, read a book—whatever makes you feel productive.

9. *Make amends.* You can use this time of your life to reflect on the people whose lives you have touched—either positively or negatively. Visit, call, or write those where a relationship has been broken. Forgive. While we each have regrets, determine that you will do everything possible to leave the world with fewer of them.

10. *Nurture your spirit.* Meditate, reflect, read the Bible, pray, fellowship. The older we get, the more difficult it is to change. Resolve that you will make adjustments. Don't give in to the false belief of "that's the way I've always been." No matter how old or young we are, there is always room for change.

Wise King Solomon wrote, "Now all has been heard: here is the conclusion of the matter: Fear God and keep his commandments, for this is the whole duty of man" (Eccles. 12:13). As Dr. Walker muses, "I'm not sure 'old age' is the best, but it's as much a part of our journey as our adolescence, and how we cope with it depends so very much on the years that precede it. The certainty through it all, weal and woe, is that God was with me."

PART

II

The Masculine Trip Wire

Anatomy of Change

CHAPTER 8

How the Women's Movement Failed Men . . . and Women

MISSY IS the product of a post-patriarchal world. She is smart, articulate, well educated . . . and independent. At thirty-eight, she grew up in a world that told her a woman could be anything a man could be, perhaps even better. The mantra was reinforced at home, in school, and in the media. She believed it. It became her truth. An engineer with plenty of spunk and determination, Missy also feels disillusionment. She feels empty inside, as if something is missing. She can't put her finger on it; she just knows it's there. Not unlike the way many middle-aged men feel, she wonders, "Is this all there is to life?"

Most women in Missy's generation are dead tired. Feminists did not consider these consequences to future generations of women and families. The parity the women's movement pushed hard to achieve has become a sword of Damocles. Women are in greater danger of heart disease, stress, and anxiety/depressive disorders than ever before. They now suffer from these maladies in nearly equal proportion to men. According to Dr. Michael

Saks, "Research finds that working wives have high rates of alcohol consumption, emotional problems, and a higher rate of suicide attempts than women who do not work."[1] The two-edged sword leaves women like Missy in a state of bewilderment, wondering silently why their hard-won independence has left them feeling so empty inside.

This is the legacy of postmodernism. It promises much but delivers little. It leaves almost nothing to satisfy the soul. It offers no benchmarks for relationships or ethics. It produces little of lasting significance. And this generation seeks desperately for meaning and significance, only to find the road map for success keeps getting revised. In a word, these women are *confused*.

The belief systems and promises of fairness leave upwardly mobile women at odds with their male bosses, unable to deal with the emotional complexity of bureaucracy with tact or diplomacy. In other words, they always expect to be hurt. They go through life distrusting, like soldiers walking the streets of Iraq, waiting for the next attack. Feminism has supplanted rationalism with a form of sexist individualism. Dr. Warren Farrell is a former board member for NOW (National Organization for Women) and author of *The Myth of Male Power*. He says, "I observed something that my feminist women friends had in common: an increasing anger toward men, a restlessness in their eyes that did not reflect a deeper inner peace."[2] While feminism decries the glass ceiling in corporate culture, and rightfully so, it ultimately fails women by pitting them against the natural aggressiveness of men. To compete in this hardscrabble environment, women must infuse themselves with masculine qualities and competitiveness. It is birthed in a gender-based inferiority complex; it pits men against women in the battle for upward mobility or position. This is a dead-end street for both sexes. It leaves a trail of suspicion at every turn, creating an ever-widening divide and distrust. The glue that holds family, corporation, or churches together is trust. For thousands of upwardly mobile women, this trust is clearly missing. It's naive to presume this problem doesn't filter into homes, relationships, or social structures (including churches). Our attitudes, no matter where they came from or whether they're true, lead to our beliefs and actions.

The radical side of the women's movement has left numerous women dissatisfied. Many withdraw into an internal world of their own making, a world that feels safe and involves little emotional risk and very little trust. They become wary of what they cannot control. They forge relationships on what works best for themselves. Predictability, control, and independence prevail. The women's movement has spawned a wariness that leaves some women feeling hollow inside. If men are confused by their role in the world today, they must wonder if the women's movement didn't inadvertently generate attitudes and behaviors that mitigate against positive male-female relations. This can surely create confusion and leave women with a Faustian bargain from which it's difficult to turn back.

Saving Private Lynch

Jessica Lynch was a blonde-haired, blue-eyed private whose biggest accomplishment was getting captured by enemy forces inside Iraq. No doubt her ordeal was traumatic, because eleven fellow members of the 507th Ordnance Maintenance Company lost their lives in the confrontation. The nineteen-year-old supply clerk from Palestine, West Virginia, quickly became an American media folk hero.

Why did Lynch receive so much attention when hundreds of male soldiers died? Did they receive the same recognition? Why Lynch? Was it because she survived hostile forces during the early days of the Iraq war? Was it that Lynch and members of her unit got lost in the desert near Nasiriya? Was it that she was the victim of an unfortunate navigational error? Or was it because Lynch was a woman?

Yes, she did survive an ambush, capture, and injury, but it was the Special Forces of men that led to her eventual rescue. They saved her life by risking their own. The picture I remember is of a male soldier carrying the injured Lynch from the hospital where she'd been held hostage.

Women took to new roles during World War II because they had to. Many had jobs in factories or filled vacancies when men went abroad. But the women's movement of the late 1960s and early 1970s was different. It was fueled by defiance. The heated demands, anger, and frustration bubbled to the surface, forcing policy changes to level the playing field. Like so many pendulum swings, it went too far.

Any sociocultural swing creates its own momentum and consequences. Feminism wasn't just about leveling the playing field. It was about evening the score. It was, and is, about putting men down—at any cost. If there are victims in the process, well, that's just too bad. After all, the reasoning goes, women have been victims for centuries, so perhaps it will do men good to see what it feels like to be second-class human beings.

Radical feminism is no less virulent than racism. It's a form of intolerance justified under the banner of equality. Robin Morgan, the editor of *MS* magazine said, "I feel that man-hating is an honorable and viable political act, that the oppressed have a right to class-hatred against the class that is oppressing them."[3] Women like Morgan are angry, and angry women are not attractive women. Understandably, some women are angry because the men in their lives have been unkind or cruel. But are some men unkind and cruel because women have become disrespectful and ugly? It's a vicious cycle of gender dysfunction fueled by suspicion. Angry women place their relationships at risk. As the Lynch story illustrates, a double standard has become the new norm in our society.

Liberation or Subjugation?

If women have been liberated, why are so many exhausted, depressed, or otherwise unhappy? To them, the answer is simple: Men are holding them back. If men would only _____ (you can fill in the blank). It's a throwback to the garden, where blame replaced responsibility. Columnist Anna Quindlen keeps the full frontal feminist attack moving at polarizing warp speed with comments such as this one: "But many of the institutions are still broken, and if they're ever to be fixed women have to keep the outsider perspective even as they sit in the big chairs, make the big deals, hold the big jobs. . . . The insiders [men] have simply made a hash of things, and everybody knows it." She is saying that no matter what women achieve, it will never be enough. An entire issue of *Newsweek* is devoted to leading women. It's as if everything men have done is wrong, and the entire world is falling apart because of their aggressiveness and pigheadedness. Quindlen quips, "There's always been the notion that if women ran the world it would be a kinder, softer, more peaceful place."[4]

In his book, *The Decline of Males*, anthropologist Lionel Tiger says, "Women's liberation has backfired. It is men who have been liberated. They needn't be husbands or fathers to assure themselves of social status. They can be ex-husbands or part-time fathers. They're not required to support women and children for life. They may experience transient social and sexual variety with a range of partners. The contemporary nuptial scheme may be problematic or seem arduous to men and hence less likely to appeal to them."[5] What Tiger is talking about is a consequence of, not an endorsement for, changes in men's behavior. It's clearly not a positive masculine quality to abandon responsibility or engage in limitless sexual adventure. But Tiger is right about the fallout from gender liberation. It cuts deeply for both men and women and fosters polarity between the sexes.

As Dorothy Kelly Patterson observed, "Men have been removed from their families, and the vacuum is being filled by a process of feminization. Masculinity has been redefined with less importance on effective fatherhood and more emphasis on personal ambition and achievement . . . strengthening families rests largely on reinvigorating the institution of fatherhood."[6]

According to Tiger, "Males have become the portmanteau cause of evil behavior that's acceptable to downgrade males. The impact on young men is that they don't know what to think or how to behave."[7] Presumably, this process of demeaning men is part of women's autonomy. I would argue this has been a Pyrrhic victory at best. More important, it has left many men confused and has adversely affected women. To an absurd extent, the very notion of appropriateness has been turned on its head. Does a man open the door for a woman or not? Does he offer to lift a heavy object, pay for a meal, or pull out a chair for a woman? Men don't know anymore. Clearly, feminism has won some victories, but women are losing the war. The women (and men) who hopped on the bandwagon of this misplaced political correctness are only now beginning to wonder if they're truly better off.

Leslie Carbone is an alternative voice on women's issues, and she writes about the impact of feminism on culture. She echoed what Tiger said with this statement: "Feminism has given ersatz moral cover for men to duck their responsibilities." Carbone went on to explain how men are socially free to abandon their families, as well as the children they've fathered out of wedlock. "Abortion has given men far more license than it has women, and often leaves them in poverty while the ex-husband just moves on."[8] The easy-divorce, low-commitment relationships leave broken hearts, broken homes, and social carnage. It's clearly not creating greater love and respect between the sexes.

Certain aspects and efforts of the women's movement have opened up new opportunity for women. Yet along with this has come entirely new pressures. Women work longer hours, have less time with their children, less free time, greater health risks, and more relationship pressures. If the relationship pressures become too much, women simply leave. After all, feminism has afforded them that option. In *Men's Passages*, author Gail Sheehy observed, "Statistically, it is women between forty and fifty-four who have been swelling the ranks of the divorced more rapidly than any other age-group since 1970. One of the unremarked revolutions of the last two decades has been the increase in professional women who find divorce a springboard and choose to remain single."[9]

One could argue that men feel emotionally or vocationally vulnerable because women are finally reaching near-parity in the workplace, thus giving them more options in relationships. In some instances, this may be true. Whether it is or not, there is no indication that the men in these women's lives *want* separation or divorce. There is no hint these men are abusive or non-supportive. What *is* evident is that these women simply make a lifestyle choice—to jettison their husbands for greener pastures. If educational and vocational opportunity equal conjugal freedom, then why stay tethered to an old tired horse? This is but one outcome of the women's movement, and it leaves many women lonely or disconnected later in life.

Not surprisingly, the rise of the women's movement coincided with two other cultural trends: the push for legalizing abortion (1973) and the sexual revolution. At about the same time, divorce was on the rise. Women (and men) found traditional values (commitment and responsibility) replaced by new values (personal freedom and happiness). As the latter supplanted the former, sexually transmitted disease and out-of-wedlock births skyrocketed. Between 1950 and 2000, the percentage of births to unmarried women rose from 4 percent to more than 33 percent.[10] The connection between these events isn't arbitrary; they happened for a reason.

American culture went through sweeping sociological change starting in the late 1960s and early 1970s. The question this generation must ask is whether women are better off today because they have access to abortion-on-demand and no-fault divorce? Therapist Teri Reisser wrote, "Like a toxic spill that can no longer be kept out of the local water supply, painful symptoms [of abortion] are now contaminating the flow in her [a woman's] daily life." Reisser explained how guilt, anxiety, depression, psychotic disorders, bonding, and fertility issues plague the 43 percent of American women who choose abortion at some point in their lives.[11] Women who choose abortion over adoption become victims of their freedom. More to the point, they're victims of the false messages force-fed to them by a women's movement bent on perpetuating misandry and fear. In the end, women who buy into these false messages become servants to their pain.

The New Meaning of Abuse and Empowerment

They were both standing in the kitchen at the time. Jerry, fifty-one, and his wife, Lisa, had two teenage boys, Josh and Rick. Jerry put his foot down about the boys' unfinished chores. Soon, Lisa's voice raised several decibels in disagreement. She was clearly frustrated that Jerry would not back down. "Why don't you go easier on the boys?" she shouted, well within earshot of her sons. She knew how important it was for them to attend the Friday night football game at John F. Kennedy High School.

Lisa slammed a pot on the counter, breaking off a piece of tile that went whizzing past Jerry's head and hit the wall. "You're a mean, hard man," she blurted as she left the kitchen mumbling. It was barely a minute later when Lisa reentered the kitchen to unload more verbal blows to her husband. Jerry braced himself for the onslaught and then reached out to grab Lisa's forearms to calm her down. It was a decision he would soon regret. Lisa pulled violently away, grabbed the phone, retreated to the guest bathroom, and locked the door. Jerry was oblivious, never imagining Lisa would call 911. Not until the police showed up at his door did Jerry "get it."

"Are you Mr. Russell?" one of the officers queried.

"Yes, I am. What's the problem, officer?"

"That's what we came to find out," he replied.

The second officer stood next to Jerry in the living room as the first officer escorted Lisa from the bathroom into the master bedroom. Ten minutes later, he came out—alone.

"Did you touch your wife?" he asked.

"Yes, I did. I tried—"

The conversation was over. The officer asked Jerry to turn around and put his hands behind his back. Jerry reluctantly complied, dazed and confused by what was happening.

He said to the officer, "You're making a big mistake."

"No," the officer barked, "you're the one who made the mistake!"

Jerry's sons watched the officers escort their dad to the squad car. Thirty minutes later, another officer took his fingerprints and a mug shot, and then placed him in a urine-stained jail cell—charging him with domestic violence. Meanwhile, the boys went to the game, and Lisa called her friends to seek support.

The benefit of the doubt in any domestic disturbance is one-sided. Since men are physically stronger, conventional logic assumes they must be guilty. Women know this, and some feel empowerment from it. Most men, even Christian men, are often victims of a distorted system that assumes they're guilty until they prove their innocence. Catherine Comins, the Assistant Dean of Student Life at Vassar College, said, "They [men] have a lot of pain, but it is not necessarily pain I would have spared them. Men who are unjustly accused of rape can sometimes gain from the experience."[12]

How are men supposed to benefit from unjust accusations? Isn't that a bit like saying, "Women can benefit from getting slapped around once in a while"? Imagine the backlash if we said that rape is "a lesson for women who dress provocatively." No one in his or her right mind would advocate such nonsense. Yet innocent men must defend themselves against false paternity suits, rape charges, and other forms of domestic abuse accusations—every day. What most men do not realize is they can be taken from their homes and kept away from their children through a no-contact order. An arrest, any arrest, leaves a man's reputation in tatters, creating doubt even if he's innocent. Meanwhile, a woman receives support and sympathy as a victim. In some cases, a man doesn't even have to lift a finger to touch his wife. He may face arrest if his wife says she *feels* threatened. Even a verbal disagreement can lead to an arrest. Since local law enforcement and prosecutors are held to exceptionally higher standards, monitored by women's advocacy groups, they're called to account if they don't arrest and prosecute men. Do you get the picture? And if you think this is an isolated example of reality, read on.

A female deputy prosecutor in my own community made a presentation to a roomful of men. Her anger was palpable as she said, "I am thankful these idiots [men] admit too much. I will bluff; I will do anything to get a plea." I wondered, for a moment, if she forgot who was in her audience. Then, alas, I realized she was so accustomed to being applauded for her ends-justify-the-means dogma, she probably didn't care. For this rural prosecutor, the truth doesn't matter. Winning a case is what's important—regardless of a man's guilt or innocence. She said, "You shouldn't always take things at face value." What is that supposed to mean? If the police and prosecutors don't take situations like Jerry's at face value and learn to use discernment, how should they handle them? The answer is they do whatever is necessary to save women from abusive men. If a few good men like Jerry are caught in the mix, well, too bad. This deputy prosecutor uses a double standard. She excuses women who hit men as using "self-defense," but says men who touch women are "abusive."[13] Men cannot win in this biased and hyper-vigilant atmosphere. It's unfortunate that this woman determines her prosecutorial strategy on an arbitrary view of what it means to be a victim. It's another confusing and irrational signal for men. And there's more . . .

Men are told, "No means No!" even in marriage. In other words, a woman can sexually arouse a man and then walk away without any explanation. Women who take their men half the way there mess with God's creative purpose. They're playing with a powerful drive. Laws that favor self-control for men but not for women protect women regardless of their behavior. It's illustrative of another double standard that creates more than mere angst; it creates resentment and distrust.

There is no question that some spouses use physical, emotional, sexual, or economic abuse. It happens. Sadly, it happens far too often. Serious abuse deserves our attention and prosecution, no matter who commits it. But frivolous charges need to stop. And men are the primary victims of these twisted charges. When overzealous or angry prosecutors are willing to bend or twist the truth to convict a man, something is seriously wrong. Conversely, in the church, there are pastors or counselors who do no favor to women by encouraging them to stay in dangerous marriages. To shame women through Scripture or guilt is unconscionable. No woman or man who leaves a genuinely abusive marriage for his or her own protection should have to defend that action. To the contrary, churches should come to the aid of such people, assisting with emotional, financial, or spiritual care.

Summer of Discontent

Harvard President Lawrence Summers is another man who made a fateful miscalculation. During an economics conference, he committed a faux pas by saying that the underrepresentation of female scientists at elite universities may stem from "innate" differences between men and women. His remarks set off a firestorm of protest that took weeks to quell.

Women make up 35 percent of faculty at universities across the country, but only 20 percent of professors in science and engineering. When Summers mentioned the "innate differences" hypothesis, he added, "I'd like to be proven wrong on this one." Yet, women's groups and the media jumped on him as if he had committed the unpardonable sin. One MIT biologist, Nancy Hopkins, said she felt physically ill.[14]

Meanwhile, women have made, and continue to make, enormous strides in every vocational and academic field. Feminist Connie Schultz doesn't think it's nearly enough. "I always told my daughter she could do anything as long as she worked hard and refused to let someone else define her" (presumably men). The truth is, though we live with a plethora of opportunities, we *can't* do anything we want. Each of us has specific skills and experiences. To tell a daughter she can be anything is to create unnecessary pressure and generate unrealistic expectations. Schultz gave a commencement address at a girls' school where she explained she was "defiant because I know that equal footing is still often an ideal caught in a chokehold with reality."[15] Christian writer Staci Eldredge admits she swallowed this misguided feminist line in college, even serving as the director of the Women's Resource Center. "But no matter how much I asserted my strength and independence as a woman ('hear me roar'), my heart as a woman remained empty. To be told when you're young and searching that 'you can be anything' is not helpful. It's too vast. It gives no direction. To be told when you are older that 'you can do anything a man can do' isn't helpful, either. I didn't want to be a man."[16]

The Schultz article replays the tired (and wrong) statistic about women earning seventy-six cents (now up to eighty cents) for every dollar a man makes for the same work. As *Ms.* magazine declares, "The average woman is cheated out of about

$250,000 in wages over a lifetime." The argument sounds good, even if it's spurious. The basis of the Census Bureau data was raw numbers not adjusted for comparable jobs and responsibility. Columnist John Leo cited work by Warren Farrell (*Why Men Earn More*) that shows when reasonable adjustments are made, women earn just as much as men, and sometimes more.[17] Men and women have been making comparable salaries for decades; it just isn't reported in the news. Women are fifteen times more likely than men to become top executives in major corporations before the age of forty. Never-married, college-educated males who work full-time make only 85 percent of what comparable women earn. Female pay exceeds male pay in eighty different fields. A female investment banker's starting salary is 116 percent of a man's. Part-time female workers make $1.10 for every dollar earned by part-time males.[18]

If men earn higher wages in certain jobs, it's largely due to the kind of jobs they take. The high risk, dangerous, or physically demanding jobs are not as glamorous. Society won't find many women applying for commercial fishing or offshore oil rigging. But the glamour, pay, and prestige are not the only issue.

The Myth of Biological Equality

Are women the weaker sex? In her book, *A Return to Modesty*, Wendy Shalit says, "Sorry, but it's true. Sexual assault is never equal opportunity." She refers to the myth of sameness and suggests we find a cure for the insecurity that seems to fuel it.[19]

Our culture, and in some cases, our churches, cannot get a handle on the difference-can-be-good paradigm. Instead of embracing our specific gender differences, they try to pretend they aren't there. But pretending never makes anything true. It just leads farther down the path toward denial. In so doing, our culture develops a warped sense of reality—one based on what we wish were true rather than on what *is* true.

Dr. James Dobson in *Bringing Up Boys* states that one over-riding difference between the sexes is testosterone. He says it's responsible, in part, for what might be called "social dominance." Dobson points out that hormonal influences not only motivate the drive for power in humans, but they also affect the way men and women relate to one another. Men have ten to twenty times more testosterone than women. This is a facilitator of risk (adventure)—physical, criminal, and personal.[20] Other studies find that on specific abilities such as verbal, quantitative, and spatial skills, there is evidence that gender differences exist. Generally, females outperform males on verbal tasks, and males do better when spatial or quantitative skills are tested.[21] While the differences are not dramatic, they're consistent.

Meanwhile, feminists refer to men as having "testosterone poisoning," a no less bigoted and false statement than to say all Hispanics are lazy. It's akin to blaming women for being "overly nurturing." Are men supposed to apologize for being created men? The effect of this nonsense is what I have already referred to in an earlier chapter, the attempt to feminize boys and men. To chide them for being . . . well, boys! Christina Hoff Sommers believes feminists want to "reform" boys. "Contrary to what many feminists say today, American boys are not deformed by societal conditioning. They do not need to be rescued. They're not pathological. They're not seething with repressed sentiments or imprisoned in 'straightjackets' of masculinity. Being a boy is not a defect in need of a cure."[22] If you think this is an overstatement, listen to how the feminist dictionary defines maleness.

> MALE: . . . represents a variant of or deviation from the category of female. The first males were mutants . . . the male sex represents a degeneration and deformity of the female.
>
> MAN: an obsolete life form . . . an ordinary creature who needs to be watched . . . a contradictory baby-man.[23]

This is incendiary hatred directed at men. It's the attitude that boys must face—and it's anti-biblical. How can women expect boys or men to grow up to take responsibility for their family if they see them as an enemy that needs to be pacified or cured?

The eradication of gender differences is a postmodern catastrophe. It has widened a gap, created polarity, and forged the mind-set—*us-against-them*—that is ruinous to relationships and families. It's hurting children, mocking inherent masculine qualities, and leaving women lonely and confused. Today's society is afraid to recognize differences where they're most obvious (among men and women). Yet, marketing is all about difference, or perceived difference. Morality is also about difference. We distinguish inferior from superior, good from evil, effective from useless, better from worse, reasonable from foolish, and so on.

That biological differences exist between men and women is not a value judgment about the dissimilarities. Instead, it should lead to mutual respect for these created differences. Our Creator put these differences in us for a reason. Certainly some of the differences are the result of humanity's rebellion or socialization, but not all. And clearly, some women have been marginalized in male-dominated cultures (see Islamic attitudes toward women). Among cultures where Judeo-Christian values have been strongest, women fare the best.

Clearly, the institution of marriage as we know it has changed more in the last thirty years than in the previous three thousand years combined. As feminist Stephanie Koontz remarked, "Marriage is harder today because it's more optional. There are more choices. The very things that make it better also make it more difficult and vice-versa."[24] Koontz falls prey to the American market myth that more choices equal better relationships. It's choice-overload. Marriage is more difficult because men and women have lost sight of their created differences. The outcome, even in Christian marriages, is that men and women engage in endless (and winless) power struggles. Is this our Creator's plan for conjugal bliss?

The Myth of Sameness
Embracing the Creator's Intent for the Sexes

ENE IS a fifty-year-old childhood friend of mine now living in Geneva, Switzerland. Though he's an American, he married a Swiss woman and has lived in Europe for fifteen years. He refers to Europe as neo-feminist. "My sense is that most who grew up with the feminist surge are beginning to grasp the opportunity cost of embracing such ideology," he explained. This has led to "a loss of comprehension of the essential maleness and masculinity. Both sexes realize something is broken in male-female relations." In Europe, though feminism is not in full retreat, it's under new scrutiny for its lack of deliverables. The women who embraced it as a panacea to their "bondage" are reconsidering the costs. The bottom line remains the same: Most women want men to be men—to be masculine. They don't want wimps, if they want men at all.

Forty-three percent of adult Americans, or 87 million, describe themselves as single. Yet, 16 percent of these 87 million Americans say they're looking for love, while 45 percent say they have no interest in a romantic partner. This feeling is especially strong among women, or those who have been divorced or widowed.[1] With the sudden increase in dating services, one would think more Americans are connecting through these services, but this may not be the case. A mere 3 percent of happy couples met online. It comes as no surprise that those least likely to care about finding a soul mate are younger singles between eighteen and twenty-nine. As far as romance is concerned, they can take it or leave it, or so they say.

Marie, another friend, is a forty-seven-year-old American woman who lives in Australia with her husband and four sons. She made this observation about the changes in male-female relationships: "Boys are trying too hard to get girls to notice them. They wear more revealing clothing, something you would never see in past generations." For her, the pressure seems abnormal. "Boys no longer seem to know who they are or what their masculinity is supposed to look like."

The question that we should be asking is this: What was God's original intent in creating male and female as separate beings? The question can raise blood pressure and frustration for both sexes, but why should people be afraid to look at what the Bible has to say? They tend to sidestep these tough questions rather than recognize that both male and female are God's creation. He made man and woman in his image. They're simply *different* in design. A healthy approach to embracing God's intention for men and women begins with losing the *us-against-them* mentality. This adversarial view is a dead end for both men and women. Let's go back and see what God said about the differences between the sexes.

Mutuality: Our Need for One Another

Men and women need one another. Can they agree on this? They may pretend they're autonomous in every sense, but this is not how God intends the sexes to relate. Feminism encourages autonomy, while God encourages dependence. There are women who hate men because their fathers, husbands, boyfriends, or bosses have been unkind; as a result, they're in pain. Feminists are in pain. However, the way to soothe our hurt is not to lash out at the source of the pain but to allow our Creator to heal the ache in our hearts. Likewise, men who resent women cannot presume to even the score by viewing them as sex objects for indiscriminate use. This only perpetuates the gender divide. It reinforces societal dysfunction, relationship distress, and gender hostility.

Even before the creation of Eve, God gave man (male) *a distinctive vocational role*. He was to work in and care for the garden. God did not create man to do nothing. He gave him a task, a purpose. Men still need a task and purpose. A man without a task is an unhappy man. Why do you think men who lose their jobs often slip into depression? It's because they feel disconnected. They feel lost. Some men become workaholics to fill a desperate need within their soul. For a man, there is an unmistakable link between his self-worth and his task. Why do so many American men die soon after they retire? If a man's tasks are taken away, he feels worthless, and often he just gives up. Clearly, men must learn to develop other interests to offset this loss. Failure to do so can lead to an emotional crisis later on.

Americans seem to have a collective inferiority complex that keeps men working far longer hours than our European counterparts. Perhaps it's a Puritan work ethic ingrained into men's psyche. Whatever the reasons, American culture sends conflicting messages to men about their tasks. It simultaneously tells men not to be lazy, to embrace a strong work ethic, while at the same time blaming them if they work too much by labeling them workaholics or accusing them of neglecting the emotional needs of the family. Our Creator understands man's desire to work, his need for a task and a purpose, but God also understands man's need for companionship—emotionally, spiritually, and physically.

After God gave Adam his work assignment (a task coupled with a purpose), he realized *something was missing* from the near-perfect picture—a compatible companion. "For Adam," the Bible tells us, "No suitable helper was found" (Gen. 2:20). What does God mean by "suitable helper"? Eve was to help Adam in every way. She was to work and care for the garden along with him. She was there to provide companionship and encouragement. There is no indication early on that Eve was physically weaker or had less endurance. This "weaker vessel" effect most likely came *after* the Fall.

God recognized that Adam needed companionship. Adam needed the woman. He still does. Why should men apologize for this need? To say that a man does not need a woman is to say God did not know what he was doing when he created Eve. Look at the separate chronology between God's creation of the man and his creation of the woman (see Gen. 2:7, 22). There is no way to know how much time elapsed between those two creative moments, only that the two human creation events were separate. The question is: Why? If God does not act arbitrarily (without a purpose), why did he wait to create the woman? Is it because he recognized the need man had *after* he created him?

If God recognized man's need for the woman, this need is not obsolete today. Man still longs for the woman. At times he tries to meet the need inappropriately, but the need remains. In the same way, the woman needs the man's strength and protection. Man's longing is the woman's affirmation of her created purpose—to be a suitable helper. Today this model is twisted and confused. Men look to the woman for strength, while the woman looks to the man for a suitable helper. I agree with John Eldredge (*Wild at Heart*) that men cannot take their cues from the woman about what it means to be a man. This is never healthy. Nor should a woman take her cues about her own femininity from the man. It doesn't work for either sex.

God brought the woman to the man (see 2:22). The woman was God's idea. The woman was God's gift to the man. She is still a gift from God to the man. Clearly, there have been distortions of these roles since the beginning. The idea behind a suitable helper is big, much bigger than the church has been willing to acknowledge. Man could not handle his duties alone; he needed help. Though he hates to admit it, he still needs help. Independence by either gender undermines the plan God set forth from the beginning. The design for men and women is that they be *partners*. This is a healthy form of mutual dependency. When a woman undermines a man's vocational role or his attempt to discipline his children, she steps outside her created purpose, and she is in rebellion. A man who fails to recognize that his wife is part of him, "bone of my bones and flesh of my flesh," rejects the gift God gives him to be his companion and helper. The man, thinking he needs no one, becomes autonomous (literally meaning "self ruler"). This is a form of idolatry directed inward.

Isn't God Sufficient?

The idea that God is not enough for *everything* seems like heresy to some Christians. The notion of God's sufficiency in all things is a rarely questioned truism, as if we're afraid to consider its veracity. This imbedded truth surfaced during a conversation I was having with a middle-aged woman. She matter-of-factly stated, "God is sufficient to meet *all* our needs." I told her it sounds good. It sounds religious. It sounds righteous. My only question to her was, "Why do you think God created Eve; wasn't God enough for Adam?"

The Bible says that God is a spirit, and he must be worshipped in spirit and in truth (see John 4:24). If God is a spirit, then how can he meet an individual's need for physical intimacy? To say he cannot doesn't make God weak or powerless. He's simply *different* in a physical sense. God understood this limitation when he created Eve to be a suitable helper. When a Christian says, "God is sufficient," I have to ask, "Sufficient for what?" People get it confused. They think it limits God when it's suggested he doesn't meet the sexual needs of human beings. He's a spirit, and that's not what spirits do. When God created Eve, he understood the difference between a physical and non-physical being. He understood Adam's need for physical intimacy. The man and woman were to become one flesh—physically. It's a part of God's design, and it appears to have worked exceedingly well since the beginning.

The lie of feminism is that Eve doesn't need a man—she needs no one but herself. The lie of the man is the same—he can make it on his own, alone. This is not an indictment on single people. It's an indictment on an attitude of rebellion against God's original purpose—togetherness, teamwork, compatibility. After the Fall, an entirely new set of divine rules and roles for the sexes became necessary to establish continuity in relationships.

After the Fall: New Roles for the Sexes

When sin entered the world, it hurt both sexes. It created disequilibrium in nature, in relationships, and in gender roles. Adam received God's judgment, but so did Eve. These role changes came directly from God. They remain controversial well into the twenty-first century and certainly fly in the face of feminist ideology. Look at how gender roles changed after sin entered the world.

Genesis 3 recounts the Fall. Skipping past the temptation and rebellion, go directly to God's response. Eve received two consequences for her sin, and Adam received one.

EVE
1. "I will greatly increase your pains in childbearing" (Gen. 3:16).
2. "Your desire will be for your husband, and he will rule over you" (Gen. 3:16).

ADAM

1. "Cursed is the ground because of you; through painful toil you will eat of it all the days of your life" (Gen. 3:17).

The controversy and intrigue has to do with the woman's second consequence. One cannot rule over someone or something of equal strength or endurance. The Fall probably created a physical disparity between the sexes. It may have existed before the Fall, but I doubt it. Overall, men are taller, stronger, heavier, develop muscle differently, and have greater capacity for endurance in nearly every activity. This difference is undeniable. The woman's desire for her husband is not without purpose. *It's for her protection.* Her physical limitations make her vulnerable. It places her at risk in a sin-filled world. One can argue that a woman no longer needs protection today, but it's a hollow argument. The Fall put man in a place of *responsibility* for his wife and family. She needed him for his protection, and she needed him for what he could provide.

He needed her for companionship and for procreation.

When a man leaves his wife or family, he makes them vulnerable (physically, spiritually, and emotionally). He (the man) is told to leave his father and mother and to cleave (adhere or be faithful to) his wife. God has a reason for this too. The marriage is a new unit or partnership that must take flight on its own—to become an interdependent unit of independence that is dependent on God. A man with divided interests (still tied to mother or father) cannot give his undivided attention or protection to the newly formed unit. Nor can a man be a protector if he's a she-man. He must be strong. He must be tough. He must be masculine! A culture that de-masculinizes boys or men leaves a woman unprotected. Meanwhile, a woman who emasculates a man leaves herself vulnerable. The woman that resists the consequences of her own Edenic rebellion finds herself alone, or with a passive-aggressive man. This man is unbalanced. He's a

poor protector. In some instances, this man becomes the problem (abuser). Instead of protecting women, he preys on them.

All You Need Is Not Love:
The Missing Link of Love and Respect

Feminism doesn't encourage women to respect men. It encourages them to respect themselves, to be independent, to take
control of their lives. Meanwhile, some men equate love and
masculinity with sexual conquest. It becomes a cycle of dysfunction, distrust, and disappointment, and it perpetuates itself. The
result is two people fighting for their right to happiness.
Ironically, in the end, neither gets it. This is not how our Creator
intends the sexes to find fulfillment in relationship.

Jason and Lisa are prime examples of what doesn't work.
Married for more than twenty years, they never left the power-
struggle stage of their relationship. Before their Christian marriage finally unraveled, both found themselves in endless debate
over children, work, finances, and sex. Lisa used sex, or lack of
it, to punish Jason. It was her way to let him know she still had
control over her body. She made sure not to give into his need.
But this controlling behavior only produces greater frustration,
anxiety, and temptation, and it eventually backfired.

Lisa took control of the children, taking on the role given by
God to the husband as protector for his family. She shared her
pain with the kids, reversed decisions made by Jason, and never
saw the destructive seed she was sowing. Lisa was poisoning the
emotional health of her marriage, all the while thinking she was
doing the right thing. Instead of stepping back to recognize what
she was doing, she kept her blinders on. Lisa said, "When I married Jason, I married for better or worse." Like many Christian
women, her marital paradigm included Jason's unconditional
love for her but not her unconditional respect for him. It was
lopsided. Lisa's understanding of a healthy marriage did not

include anything about her desire being for her husband. Nor did it include anything about his protective covering for her or their children in their home.

Author Staci Eldredge explained what a man needs to hear from his wife. She said to tell him that you "need him and believe in him. That is what a man needs to hear from his woman more than anything else. I need you. I need your strength. I believe in you. You have what it takes."[2] A man needs to hear these words from his wife. The Creator's intent is that husband and wife fill the emotional and physical void through mutual love, empathy, and kindness. Why is it so difficult to say the words *I need you*?

The marriage between feminist ideology and rebellion pushes men away from women, at least in an emotional sense. There is a world of difference between a strong woman and an emotionally unavailable woman. If Christian women want husbands who love them, they must speak the words their man needs to hear. Men cannot sense what women don't say. Men cannot discern what's in a woman's heart or mind. Women want men to understand them, instinctively. When a woman withdraws or becomes annoyed at her husband's inability to understand her heart, she stirs up insecurity and frustration in him.

As Lisa withdrew her love and respect, Jason felt rejection. Men take a woman's refusal for sexual intimacy as a declaration of war. A woman's refusal triggers a man's deepest insecurities about rejection. On a primal or unconscious level, she is saying, "You're not worthy," "You're not good enough," "I don't want you," "You aren't enough of a man for me." Christian men want and need more from their wives. The tired feminist mantra of "my body, my choice" has infiltrated Christian marriage in a way that destabilizes the relationship at its most vulnerable point.

Jason says that Lisa heard nothing he said about the core issues of their relationship. Does this sound familiar? Typically it's the woman who says, "He just won't listen. I can't get him to talk to me. He never hears my heart." This sad story works in both directions. Many Christian women and some Christian men live in a fairytale world. "He won't leave me," she reasons, "because he's obligated to love me unconditionally."

I will repeat what I said in an earlier chapter: *Unconditional love is an ideal. Every human relationship has conditions.* Husbands and wives must strive to meet those conditions if the relationship is to function effectively—if at all. But to deny the conditionality within marriage is to ignore the obvious and hide behind false idealism.

Lisa acted upon her belief system, namely, that she could behave anyway she wanted without the ensuing consequences. Unconsciously she was saying, "I don't have to have sex with him if I don't want to. I don't have to show Jason respect around the children if I don't want to. I don't have to respond to what he says is important to him because he must love me unconditionally." A statement from Dr. Emerson Eggerichs, quoted in an earlier chapter, bears repeating: ". . . the cold, hard truth is that men are often lured into affairs because they're sexually deprived at home. A man who strays is usually given total blame for his affair, but in many cases he's the victim of temptation that his wife helped bring upon him."[3]

If a man's emotional or sexual bank account is empty, what is he supposed to do? Does he go for counseling? Should he give his need to God? Should he channel his frustration elsewhere? If his wife is unresponsive, he has a problem, but it's not just his problem. It's *their* problem. Our Creator put this drive within the man. It's the Creator's intent that the man's sexual drive finds an outlet within the context of his marital relationship. If his wife refuses, she must accept part of the blame if he looks elsewhere to find the fulfillment that God has assigned her to provide within the context of a godly marriage. (Of course, for a man to look elsewhere is not what God planned at all.)

Eventually, Jason withdrew. He gave up on the relationship, a sign that his marriage was in deep trouble. Lisa was oblivious to the seriousness of the problem because she lived within her fairytale world. The breakdown in most Christian marriages is mutual. Certainly, there are instances where one person shoulders greater blame. Still, ownership of responsibility is a critical step toward restoration. Acknowledging we're wrong, inadequate, or deficient is difficult. It's tough work to change attitudes, belief systems, or behavior. In a relationship, it's always easier to view the other person as guilty, rather than admit responsibility, regardless of how small one may think it is. Making change is an act of courage, and it's never easy.

God Save the Queen:
When Government Becomes Protector

In his book, *The Myth of Male Power*, Dr. Warren Farrell includes an entire section (five chapters) about how the government has become a substitute husband. Of course, some women will say the men in their lives have not been there for them, and so the government stepped in by default. But if these men have not been there to provide or to protect their wives or children, the remedy may be worse than the disease. God never gave a government the right or responsibility to fill the role he designed for husbands and fathers. One can say the government takes on financial or legal responsibility because men do not. I would argue the government's role, if there is one, is to hold men accountable to meet their obligations instead of enabling them to flee from their responsibilities.

When the government gets involved, the outcome is rarely favorable for men. When it comes to incarceration, rape, sexual or domestic abuse, the tables are disproportionately lopsided. Men and women on an equal basis are likely to initiate domestic violence at every level of severity.[4] Yet 90 percent of the police reports are made by women about men. Here, too, men feel they cannot win, that the odds are stacked against them. Society expects men to "suck it up" and take it like a man. If there is an arrest, and a man and a woman are involved in the same crime, the man serves time while the woman gets probation. Local governments step in to provide legal and financial assistance for the woman, while the man must figure it out on his own. How many shelters for a battered man have you seen? I rest my case.

When government becomes the surrogate husband or father, a man feels displaced in his God-given role as protector and provider. It's no wonder a man gives up, flees, and lets government agencies take on his burden. It's not the government's role to displace a man. When a man fails in his duty to spouse or children, the church and not the government needs to step in. As a church, Christians have neglected their spiritual role of caring for widows and orphans and have handed it over to the government. The unintended result of the government's interference and the church's failure is that men feel they can leave their families with little effect on themselves.

In many states and cities, the police now have a mandatory policy of arresting a man in a suspected abuse case, even when there is no evidence of abuse and even when the woman refuses to press charges.[5] This is an unreasonable and egregious double standard. The bias plays out in the courts too. The legal system presumes the man is guilty for certain crimes (sex and domestic violence) until he proves his innocence. By accepting government's intrusion into our homes and marriages, the church relinquishes God's original role for protection and authority within the home.

While the notion of man as protector seems old-fashioned, it clearly has its sociological and spiritual purpose. The weak and helpless need society's protection for the aged, the infirm, and, yes, women. No woman wants to view herself as dependent or feeble yet some clearly are. Since individuals see themselves as part of a "can-do" culture, they prefer not to admit their need for anything or anyone. Pride and delicacy keep them from embracing God's intention for male-female relations.

As Robert Bly wrote, "The fading of the warrior contributes to the collapse of civilized society. A man who cannot defend his own space cannot defend women and children."[6] Culture today pacifies the warrior-man, rendering him helpless. It's small wonder that a man feels lost, struggling through the dark spaces of life, devoid of compass and bereft of direction. He's numb from disuse, looking for a purpose, yearning for respect.

Finishing Touches: Distinction of Favor

God created man and woman in his image. He created moral beings with the ability to choose between right and wrong, prudence or foolishness, love or disdain. God would have it no other way. How could he find a way to encourage men and women to honor and obey him without compelling them to do so? How could he encourage men and women to love and respect one another without forcing them to do so? Freedom inevitably necessitates choice, and choice is ultimately a creative act. The Bible says, "He [God] created him [mankind]; male and female he created them" (Gen. 1:27). The implication in this passage is the distinction between the sexes—distinct, yet compatible and alike. This is how God wanted it.

In the twenty-first century, humankind seeks to eradicate differences. This is nothing more than "gender-bending." The unisex, metero-sexual world is a kaleidoscope of cross-dressing, gender-neutral, bisexual experiences that rouse confusion. The deconstruction of gender differences is evidence of our tinkering with the Creator's intent in design. Gender-bending removes differences (on the presumption that they're wrong) and encourages transgendering. In other words, a person thinks he or she can become anything he or she wants by personal fiat. In this Alice in Wonderland–like world, these choices become godlike creations where a person's will overrides God's design, and perversity supplants moral clarity. In this muddle of dysfunction, God's intended role between the sexes gets lost in a smoky haze.

"When the Lord created humankind," wrote author Francis Frangipane, "He placed unique graces in man and separate but equally unique graces in woman." The naming of the animals brought order and structure to the human experience, and it also tells us something about the man's organizational and administrative capacity. As Frangipane said, "He [Adam] defined reality."[7] The man with his administrative ability and the woman with her creative abilities made for a powerful duo. The very name "Eve" means "Life." There is no hint that Adam felt weakened by the presence of Eve or that Eve felt deprived because she did not receive Adam's organizational abilities.

Author Dorothy Kelly Patterson wrote that the woman is identified as one "comparable to him [the man]. She is like and equal to the man in her person even though different from him and unique in her function." Patterson also explained, "The woman was neither inferior nor superior to the man, but she corresponded to him in such a way as to make it possible for them to have the most intimate fellowship. In the midst of difference in nature and function, women and men need to be conscious of what each can do to respond to the needs of the other."[8]

We respond to the needs and desires of one another when we give ourselves away physically or emotionally. In the physical act, we become mutually vulnerable, finding release (physically, emotionally, and spiritually) through relinquishing control. As a result, we find both euphoria and relaxation in the release. For a woman, the act of sex itself is one of vulnerability, openness, and acceptance. Do you see it? *Our differences become our greatest source of joy.* For the man it's an act of giving himself to the woman—releasing his strength into her body. The Creator's intent for a man and a woman is that they recognize the differences and celebrate them for what they are—God's design.

Media Madness
How the Media Marginalizes
Men and Fathers

WHY ARE men the butt of so many jokes, the laughing-stock of countless television sitcoms? What makes men such an easy target for ridicule and scorn by producers, writers, and authors? The anti-male bias keeps growing, and it shows few signs of fading anytime soon. Men make the perfect target because they're taught not to whine. As Warren Farrell says, "Men put their heads in the sand and hoped the bullets would miss!"[1] Men are supposed to be tough guys who wear emotional flak jackets. They're supposed to take countless arrows and never get dented. The truth is just the opposite; men do get hurt. The barrage of disparaging messages penetrates deep within the soul. And any message that is repeated often enough leaves a man wondering if the messages *could* be true.

Anti-fathering books like Maureen Dowd's *Are Men Necessary: When Sexes Collide* and Peggy Drexler's *Raising Boys without Men* only serve to further diminish men—and boys.

Drexler believes that masculinity arises naturally, which makes having a father around little more than a nuisance. But her premise is faulty. Boys do not grow to become responsible men through genetic causality. The countless lost boys and men in our culture attest to the fact that masculinity is something deeper than biology. Genuine Creator-centered masculinity is nurtured and learned.

Drexler believes men are bullies, dads too demanding, and fathers abusive. When an individual starts with negative assumptions based on false deductions, these stereotypes stick. As Caitlin Flanagan, a reviewer for *The New Yorker*, wisely notes, "Belittle men's responsibilities to their families, raise boys to believe that fatherhood is not a worthy aspiration, and the people who will suffer are women and children."[2] For this astute reviewer, the long-term consequences of media madness are more than a dead-end street, they're a catastrophe. "For the past forty years," wrote Flanagan, "women have been insisting that they be able to enjoy the same sexual freedom as men (you go, girl!), and to become single mothers by choice (ditto!). Surprise, surprise, men have been more than happy to comply. Some day American women may realize that the great achievement of civilization . . . was convincing men that they had an obligation to contain their sexual energies within marriage, and to support—economically and emotionally—the children they created in that marriage."[3]

Meanwhile Dowd, unmarried and childless, appears to use her book as a personal excuse to bash men. She believes most men are too emotionally fragile to handle powerful women. That men are put off by strong women and prefer women who will serve them. Dowd has it half right. Everyone wants someone to serve them. This is not a male or female trait; it's a human one. No doubt, strong, intelligent women in positions of power intimidate some men in much the same way that some women are unsettled by powerful men. Most men care less about the gender-power connection than the power-fairness or competency connection. Dowd seems to revel in a zero-sum game of male bashing. As *Slate* reviewer Katie Roiphe penned, "Dowd's aphorisms, amusing and pithy in the morning paper along with a cup of coffee, are precisely what the conversation about sexual politics does not need."[4]

The negative reviews notwithstanding, most of them by women, point not to a valid sociological issue but rather to how the media carries messages that reinforce polarity between the sexes. To heal the rift, these messages must become prescriptive rather than increasingly caustic. Destruction is far easier than construction. The latter takes time, skill, and ingenuity; the former requires only hatred. The media fans the flames of social unrest because they're more interested with winning the ratings game than in maintaining a workable society. Ratings and sales are the name of the game. If this were not so, there would be far more positive than negative news. Our culture wallows in the sensational, the shocking, and the bizarre. Perhaps it's an omen for a society on the brink of imploding.

The degree to which society's appetite for celluloid stimulation grows, their impatience with the ordinary diminishes. Individuals have lost their immunity to what used to shock or entertain them, and the media know this. It's called desensitization. Continually pushing and expanding the boundaries of civility is like filling a balloon with too much air. In time, the entire support structure weakens. Sixty years ago, shortly after the Second World War, Maureen Dowd's title would have made her a laughingstock. Were men necessary? The European continent knew they were. Women knew they were. A grateful nation knew they were. Today, however, we allow doubts to linger, like helium-filled balloons around a fire. This nonsense under the guise of free speech misses the point of prudence and truthfulness.

Conservatives have long blasted the media for being too liberal but fail to explain what this means. If the media is too liberal, how does their liberalism affect men, women, or families?

As a political philosophy, liberalism advocates personal freedom and thereby reduces rigidity. In the moral arena, personal freedom can easily supplant social restraint. It can, and often does, confuse traditional values with shackling freedom. This is where the media gets it wrong. They often assume, falsely, that all ideas espoused by any vocal tribe are equally worthy. The truth is that not all ideas or philosophies are of equal value. A person need look no further than Nazism to make this point. Ideas have consequences. Beliefs formed from ideas have consequences. When liberal media push fringe ideas, like those of Dowd and Drexler, they get coverage. To suggest that all ideas have equal value, as many liberals do, is sentimentalism run amuck. The ideological stepchildren to this belief are tolerance and diversity. They're worthy aspirations when directed toward ethnic imbalances but dubious as a moral philosophy. To be tolerant of *any* belief system or viewpoint is the pendulum swing of a culture that has lost sight of truth, prudence, and healthy boundaries.

Bill Proctor, a Harvard Law graduate and former reporter for the *New York Daily News*, says the media is anything but unbiased. This bias is evident in books, magazines, television, movies, and the news. "When any news organization elects to become an advocate for a particular political or social viewpoint rather than be a detached observer and reporter, balance becomes impossible,"[5] wrote Proctor. Though there are cries about the impartiality of Fox News, the media is overwhelmingly not conservative. A whopping majority (97 percent) of journalists are pro-abortion. Eighty-nine percent of the reporters at the *New York Times* voted for Bill Clinton in 1992, and on issues like adultery, homosexuality, and abortion, a disproportionate number of journalists are strongly in favor.[6]

It's axiomatic that people today cannot see their own biases, weaknesses, or problems like others do. This paradox forces individuals to gravitate toward those who hold similar biases. Church people are not immune to this any more than liberals in the media or education. Yet lack of objectivity is no excuse for failure to act responsibly. Media that directly or indirectly stirs the pot of male antipathy invites the unavoidable consequences that weak or angry men bestow on culture. Perhaps nowhere are men more a target for ridicule than during prime-time television.

Prime-Time Bashing

Take a moment to think about some of the recent past and present television sitcoms or movies. Do they depict men as kind, intelligent, thoughtful husbands or fathers? Go back as far as the family-friendly *Home Improvement*, starring bumbling comedian Tim Allen. Tim "the-tool-man" Taylor was a clumsy idiot. Jill, his wife, went to college to better herself and spent much of her time trying to keep her inept husband from hurting himself or others. The message from *Home Improvement* is that men may have good intentions, but they're clueless at life. And this is the message from what many consider one of the better programs.

Meghan Caldwell discussed male bashing in her article for *Ethics Monthly*: "The male-bashing trend has been growing slowly," observed Caldwell, "but in the last five years it has accelerated to the point that men in sitcoms can depend upon being humiliated. Where men used to have a stereotype of being strong, stern, macho, they now have become stereotyped as lazy, stupid, ignorant."[7]

The animated *Simpsons* introduced another bumbling, overweight idiot named Homer. Even his son, Bart, though obviously deficient in his own way, was more in touch with reality than his dad. Meanwhile, high-haired mom, Marge Simpson, kept her husband's feet on the ground. She maintained the emotional equilibrium of the family while accepting her husband in spite of his idiocy. Without the woman in his life, Homer was lost. His favorite activities of drinking beer, watching television, and eating donuts played into unhelpful stereotypes.

Another family-friendly program, *Everybody Loves Raymond*, perpetuates the myth that men are dense. The father and brother, as well as Raymond, just aren't playing with a full deck. They may be kind, but they don't really understand the real world. Most sitcoms treat men like children. These men need their women to take them by the hand and walk them through life. No doubt, some men fill their free time drinking beer, polishing their hunting rifles, attending monster truck events, or watching championship wrestling. However, as media increasingly stereotypes men negatively, we collectively come to believe these representations to be the norm. They are not. Not all men are sexists, rapists, abusers, or users who drool when they see a beautiful woman walk by.

Not all fathers are deadbeat dads who need help interpreting what it means to love, care, lead, or protect their families. In his book, *Bringing Up Boys*, Dr. James Dobson addresses media portrayals of men in a chapter titled "Men R Fools." Dobson observed, "Masculine virtues such as moral character, self-control, integrity, and confidence rarely show up in a dramatization . . . women on the other hand, come off as hard-nosed, physically powerful professionals, usually lawyers or surgeons, who are in control."[8] In another article, *Is Your Son Glad to Be a Boy?*, Dobson said positive male role models are almost nonexistent; instead, the media consistently show an anti-masculine bias.[9]

If boys and men feel lost in today's culture, the media only reinforces the unconscious message that men can never quite measure up—they will always be stupid, lazy, or abusive. If this is what culture wants from men, nothing should be done to stop it— just keep the myths coming at lightning speed and at every turn. By capitulating to such a destructive attitude, it won't take long until it becomes a self-fulfilling prophecy. Most women I know don't want weak men. They want men who work hard, love their kids, and lend an ear. Most women want a man with traditional values, engaged, enlightened, and sensitive. They don't want the men they see in sitcoms. If these are the best that women can hope for, it's no wonder they begin to ask, "Are men necessary?"

The negative stereotyping is yet another paradox. Men develop 75 percent of shows on TV, and they write two-thirds of them.[10] Robert Bly has his own theory about male bashing by the broadcast media. About situation comedies he said, "Men are devious, bumbling, or easy to outwit. It's the women who outwit them, and teach them a lesson, or hold the whole town together by themselves." Bly believes "many young Hollywood writers would rather confront their fathers indirectly by taking revenge on the remote father by making all adult men look like fools."[11] Whether this assessment is correct may be hard to prove, but if he's right, a lot of hurt, angry men and women—mostly from broken and uncaring families—are on the loose. If they generalize their anger outward, they take a non-redemptive approach to remedying their pain, and like all false solutions, their relief is short-lived. Hollywood writers and producers need reminding that strength and abuse are not synonymous.

The "nitwitification of American Men," as Ross Parker and Armin Brott call media bashing in their book *Throwaway Dads*, leaves an emotional residue both individually (on men) and collectively (on society). They observe the media doing more harm than good in getting fathers to take responsibility as active parents. "Hammering men over the head—and so wildly exaggerating—their shortcomings only fills them with feelings of shame that drive them further from their families."[12] Shame does not motivate men. In boys, shame often turns to resentment. Shame is a method of controlling and manipulating men and boys. Those who use this form of "punishment" find themselves empty and alone—through silence ("My man won't talk to me"), abandonment ("Who needs this?"), violence ("I've had it!"), or capitulation ("I'll do anything you want me to"). None of these misplaced responses solves anything in relationships. They may in fact produce the opposite effects. A woman who uses shame to control her son or husband is essentially taking on the role of the Holy Spirit, whose role it is to convict of sin. Shame-based control instills guilt—often false guilt. This can add to a man's already overburdened sense that he can't, or doesn't, measure up.

Undercurrents of Anti-Family Bias

It's simple enough to see how the media portrays men as oblivious or ignorant. What is not seen is what's happening on a subterranean emotional level. Faulty messages, even those done in jest, tear at the fabric of family. American culture has devolved into a 3,500-mile-wide coliseum any night of the week. The theater of America is bursting with television, computers, and games, all of which consume copious amounts of time. And parents, especially dads, end up with almost no quality or quantity time with their children, and this is not exclusively their fault.

When children between the ages of two and five spend an average of twenty-two hours a week in front of the TV, two questions must be asked: First, who or what is instilling values in our children? Second, how can fathers compete with the fast-moving, mind-numbing images?

Electronic-based media and games rob fathers of time with their children—even the babies, since the advent of the "Baby Channel"! Certainly, parents must decide how much time their children should spend in front of a TV or computer in their home, but it's worth considering the fact that in the precious few homes where television is not present, kids do better in school. They also do better in social relationships. Those who are allowed to consume countless hours of media inevitably experience the residual effects of exposure to violence, bad language, sarcasm, or messages that contradict biblical or moral truths. In other words, too much media exposure undermines rather than builds respect for authority, relationship, or family.

The anti-family bias manifests itself through distractedness, and a distracted child is a socially disengaged child. By limiting the distractions in the home, a father hits the reset button with his children. He needs time for interaction, for games, for reading, for engagement. When my own sons were small and we lost power during a heavy wind or snowstorm, off went the television, computers, and lights, and out came the candles, flashlights, and lanterns. My sons loved it. They liked it so much they wanted to simulate the loss of power, pretending we had to spend the night making light with batteries and matches. What we did during those times was tell stories (often scary ones) or play board games. My point is this: kids want something more than the world has to offer. Though most kids crave relationship with their dads, many boys do not get enough one-on-one time with them, and some get none at all.

The challenges with media are not just the anti-fathering biases. Recent generations that have grown up on television or computers show pervasive deficiencies in social and community skills. In her book, *The Plug-In Drug*, Marie Winn writes, "The relationships of family members to each other are affected by television's powerful competition in both obvious and subtle ways. For surely the hours that children spend in one-way relationship with television people, an involvement that allows for no communication or interaction, must have some effects with their relationships on real-life people."[13] Winn and others point out the importance of eye-to-eye contact in normal human relations. Children whose only means of understanding human relations is through electronic media can end up with distorted relational skills. They develop warped ideas about male-female relationships, violence, work, and problem solving. Fathers have always been the primary teachers about how to handle conflict, self-control, work, or the opposite sex. When boys pick up their cues from the media, they usually get it wrong. And when they internalize the "man-is-stupid" idea, they withdraw or act out. This polarity of response means they either become angry and controlling or silent and reserved. In either case, women are not attracted to these imbalances in men.

In *Habits of the Heart*, social researcher Robert Bellah wrote, "They [the media] do not support any clear set of beliefs or policies, yet they cast doubt on everything . . . the debunking that is characteristic of our intellectual culture is also characteristic of the mass media. While television does not preach it, it nevertheless presents a picture of reality that influences us more than an overt message could."[14] It's this covert message that hits boys and men the hardest. It infiltrates the home and is as hard to clear away as a toxic spill. When Bellah talks about casting doubt on everything, he's right. This negative media message produces an undercurrent of cynicism, and cynicism robs us of motivation. Instead of seeing the world for all its wonder and excitement, we begin to see only storm clouds. And far from being unbiased, the media has both its favorites (women and gays) and least favorites (men and Christianity).

In his book simply titled *Bias*, former CBS insider Bernard Goldberg uncovered a score of these biases—included in a chapter titled "Targeting Men." He cites one example from the NBC *Today* show. In a *Today* interview, Katie Couric, asked a bride who had been jilted at the altar about a proper remedy: "Have you considered castration as an option?" Imagine if cohost Matt Lauer had turned the question around to a jilted groom: "Have you considered the option of cutting off her breasts?" It would cost Lauer his job, and rightfully so. Goldberg observes that there are whole segments on the news about breast cancer—but hardly a word about prostate cancer. Yet men have a higher risk (33 percent) of contracting cancer of the prostate than women have of contracting breast cancer.[15]

The anti-male bias in the media is not just about traditional roles or responsibilities; it's deeper than that. The newer, assertive, aggressive roles for women in television and movies are astounding, as women fill numerous heroic and risk-taking roles. This is not to say women cannot be heroic; the trend, however, is for men to watch these super-women do their thing—fictionally, heroically, skillfully. These women are by-products of the feminist surge. These I-can-make-it-on-my-own types often equate happiness with independence, which is a farce. Independence only breeds loneliness and eventual despair. Recent television programs like *Grey's Anatomy*, *Crossing Jordan*, *Alias*, *Dark Angel*, *Buffy the Vampire Slayer*, *ER*, *Law and Order*, and *CSI* show women as hero-types. In many of today's movies, women play mythological or modern-day heroes—*Charlie's Angels*, *Cat Woman*, *Alien*, *Electra*, "Storm" in *X-Men*, and *Species* are but a few examples. In their book, *Same Difference*, Roselind Barnett and Caryn Rivers talked about women in the media. "Women are moving at astonishing speed and in large numbers into what used to be exclusively male turf. They're being told that there's nothing they can't achieve; and they should 'Just Do It!' These days the female of the species is more deadly than the male—at least in Hollywood's eyes."[16]

While the media builds women into *über* heroes, it concurrently tears men down, showing them powerless to rescue a damsel in distress, let alone themselves—this despite the fact that there are countless real-life examples of ordinary men who serve as heroes. When society creates fictional portrayals of women's physical abilities, they inadvertently place the women in greater physical jeopardy by leading them to believe they can overwhelm men.

What are the solutions to male bashing in the media?

First, Christian men and women need to recognize the seriousness of what's happening, that is, what is this new generation of young boys learning about being a man by watching a man make a fool of himself on television? This is clearly not a good thing for men or for society. It's not good for women either, since having weak or angry men around only increases women's vulnerability.

Second, Christians must reject negative stereotypes of men and replace them with positive and true images of men by focusing on strong, masculine role models, rather than on exclusively cynical examples.

Third, we must recognize that so-called "family-friendly" programs do not necessarily send positive or accurate messages about men and boys.

Fourth, we need to monitor every form of media allowed in the home. Identify overt and unfair biases—point them out, talk about them, reject them as being the anti-family messages that they are.

PART

III

Reclaiming Masculinity

Beyond the Myth of Invincibility

CHAPTER 11

What Do Men Need Most?

J EREMY AND his wife, Sara, were in crisis. For two long years, Sara refused to show any love or affection, and Jeremy was feeling anger and rejection. Though she had never been particularly affectionate, sexually or otherwise, Jeremy was just the opposite. He needed more than Sara was willing or capable of giving. Worn-out and emotionally exhausted, he called a female therapist with a local Christian counseling agency. By the time Jeremy and Sara arrived for their initial appointment, both were doing their best to avoid one another at home. The tension was building, and their teenage sons felt the icy chill.

The therapist turned to Jeremy and asked why he had come to counseling. He reached into his pocket and pulled out a list of items he believed had plagued his marriage. The therapist's eyes widened, as if Jeremy's writing down his concerns were taboo. He described how their sexual relationship had gone from next to nothing to nothing. He said he felt detached, frustrated, and exhausted. The therapist then asked a question that struck Jeremy as odd, if not completely out of place: "If your wife were sick or unable to meet your need for sexual intimacy, wouldn't you still love her?" Jeremy was bewildered by the irrelevance of the question and replied, "Of course I would, but she's *not* sick or an invalid." Jeremy then reversed the question by asking the therapist, "Do you think your husband would be okay with it if you decided not to have sex with him—indefinitely?" When she reluctantly admitted that he would not be okay with it, he said, "It's not okay with me either."

While sex is important to most men, it's not the only issue that can drive a wedge between men and women. There are eight fundamental needs that most men want met in their primary relationship. While no relationship is perfect, when a woman pretends these needs don't matter, her relationship is headed for trouble. If you're a woman reading this you might be thinking, "Hey, I have needs too. What about my needs?" And that is a fair question, but since this book deals with boys and men, this chapter emphasizes what a man needs and desires from the woman he loves. A woman can ignore any one of these needs, but sooner or later it will put the relationship at risk. It will create a weak point in the marriage, and wherever your marriage wall is weak, that vulnerability is precisely where the enemy will concentrate his greatest effort.

With this said, the inverse is also true. Author Gordon MacDonald states that an unguarded strength becomes a double weakness. A couple can ill afford to leave sections of their marriage walls vulnerable and untended. The surreptitious nature of the adversary is to try to breech these walls and infiltrate where it's least expected. Now, let's go back to Jeremy and Sara for a moment. Sara ignored one of the most obvious needs that every man has.

1. A man needs physical intimacy. This is not just about sex. Some women refuse to touch their man because they believe men equate a touch to sex. In some instances, this may be true, but not always. Men are no different from women in that they want someone to hold, touch, kiss, or caress them. This is not just a

male or female need; it's a human need. To love and be loved in
return is a marvelous gift that husbands and wives have to freely
offer each other. Why do couples withhold good when it's within
their power to give it? Why do they allow pettiness and power
struggles to become places that take up permanent emotional
residence?

For a man, physical intimacy also means *acceptance.* It says,
"You're worthwhile, valuable, and enjoyable." A refusal to
touch also sends men a signal that says, "You disgust me. I
want nothing to do with you." This rejection strikes at the very
heart of a man and drives pain into his soul. And it may last for
years. It can affect his sense of self and his ability to respond to
his wife's needs. This sense of rejection acts like an emotional
toxin that can eventually destroy the marriage. I understand
that most women prefer an emotional connection before giving
themselves to their husband, and this emotional heart-link is
always best. Yet when she withholds physical touch or sex simply because she doesn't "feel" that link, she places her relationship in danger.

Dr. Emerson Eggerichs stated, "Some wives want their emotional needs met after marriage but somehow lose sight of their
husband's sexual needs."[1] Again, a woman who withholds sex
as punishment or a means to exercise control sows the seeds of
resentment in her man. God created men and women to give and
receive love from one another. That is his design; it's not something nature or humanity dreamed up.

2. A man needs encouragement. A man can do great things if
he has a woman he loves in his corner. Conversely, a man can
go astray, or never reach his potential, his dreams, or his goals
if he's with a critical, controlling, shaming, or demanding wife.

Bill is a successful, self-employed electrician. He's fifty-seven
years old but looks fifteen years younger. He's a hardworking
type-A man's man. He and his wife, Linda, have two grown boys
and a nice home. Perhaps knowing what I do about Bill, his

comments to me were even more surprising. Bill, Linda, and I were standing in a small side room during a party for a friend when he said, "I feel like a loser." His wife suddenly chimed in, "Honey, I've told you; you're not a loser." Then she said something else that caught my attention, "Maybe if I tell you you're a loser, you'll stop calling yourself that." I wanted to tell her it doesn't work like that for most men, but of course, I didn't.

I had always thought of Bill as a guy doing things right—faithful, hardworking, fit, a risk-taker, a decent father, and a regular churchgoer. So why did he feel like a loser? From my vantage point, it made little sense. After talking with dozens of men, I now realize many men feel as Bill does—unworthy. I can try to analyze all the reasons Bill feels the way he does, but the bottom line is this—it isn't going to change what's going on inside of him. Many well-meaning Christians will read this and think, "Gee, Bill needs to put his trust and security in God." Maybe, but we can't discount Bill's feelings that easily. His feelings are valid for the plain and simple fact that they're his. He's a tough guy, and no one would pick him out of a crowd as being weak or insecure. Even so, the feelings of insecurity linger.

A wife can build up or tear down her husband. Her encouragement can take many forms—verbal, emotional, vocational, or physical. A man becomes a greater man when his woman stands beside him and believes in him. To need encouragement does not make a man weak or insecure. Insecurity is part of the human condition. And a man, whether he's fifteen or fifty-seven, will have to deal with insecurity in life and relationships. He must get used to the reality of the feelings, not try to diminish or be embarrassed by them.

While a male's insecurities should not define him, he shouldn't pretend he doesn't have them either. This is dishonesty, and it leads to false pride. A man hides behind many vices and masks in an attempt to avoid admitting what he knows is true, deep within his soul. Men are fallible, weak, limited, and dying. The sooner they understand and accept this, the better off they will be, and the more productive they will be for our Creator's purposes.

This is also true of a woman, who can be just as broken as the man in her life. This broken woman seems incapable or unwilling to encourage her mate. She's angry, unhappy, or insecure herself—some with good reason. And how can she give to another if she's empty herself? How can she deposit goodness and encouragement when she only feels discouragement and despair?

An invisible, God-pleasing energy flows from within when our mate stands beside us, but the opposite is also true. An unkind word, gesture, or look can affect our mood for a day—or longer. It can sap our motivation and make us feel like giving up.

George, a forty-eight-year-old man, said this about his relationship with his wife: "I'd describe my wounds as having my spirit crushed week in and week out. When I'd work all day doing a landscaping project for her, she would just redo it the way she preferred and never say a thing. I can't figure it out. All I know is I did my best 99 percent of the time, and it was never nearly good enough."

Why should anyone be surprised when relationships like this come unglued? Men are no different from anyone else in terms of their need for verbal affirmation. Verbal encouragement builds confidence and self-esteem. It costs nothing to recognize what's true and good in one another. So why isn't it done? Why aren't seeds of health and goodness sown into one another? It does takes a little effort, but the returns are so, so great.

3. *Men need forgiveness*. A marriage without forgiveness is a marriage doomed to fail. Forgiveness is the glue that holds two imperfect people together. A forgiving heart is not oblivious to hurt. It doesn't try to "pretend away" the pain, but neither does it hold on to past hurts. The key to forgiveness is in letting go of our right to be hurt. Many people find this next to impossible, and it is, without God's help. Couples must begin to see forgiveness as a cooperative effort between God and themselves.

They choose to forgive, and God unleashes a miracle in their hearts. A husband needs forgiveness from his wife and a wife needs forgiveness from the husband if the relationship is going to make it.

Matt has been married more than twenty years. In all that time, he never knew his wife, Lori, held a secret resentment toward him. What was she holding inside her heart? Matt had attended a Christian school long before he and Lori became engaged. At the school, he met a girl and stayed in contact with her for several years. He visited her family home, and they talked on the phone. Although Lori knew Matt at the time, they weren't dating nor engaged. Yet twenty years after they were married, Lori remained resentful. This kind of unforgiveness is anti-biblical. It's an unwillingness to submit one's fears or hurts to the one who can bring healing. When you fail to forgive others for past wrongs, or perceived wrongs, it builds up spiritual "gunk" in your hearts. Over time, this gunk stifles the flow of normal, healthy relations. In Matt's case, there is no way he could have guessed what Lori was holding inside all those years. And he shouldn't have had to. Lori should have been honest with him—and with herself.

Unforgiveness robs a man and woman of the joy that could be theirs. Nothing good results when a couple holds on to past hurt. It only eats up their insides like a cancer. Unforgiving people wear the strain of their secret-carrying on their faces, and they refuse to let it go.

Most people don't gravitate toward those who lack the skills to forgive. Instead, they avoid them. Lifelong carriers of resentment often feel a right to be hurt. If you ask them, they may explain the reasons why they hold on to their bitterness. To an outsider looking in, the justification makes little sense. To the unforgiving, their rationale becomes their reality.

4. *A man needs support.* This is not the same as encouragement, though the two are related. Every husband wants to know that he and his wife are on the same team, that she isn't sabo-

taging him behind his back. But it does happen! I stood in line at Wal-Mart one day and saw an elderly woman unleash a barrage of criticism and contempt at her husband. Although people were standing around her, she didn't seem to notice. Either she didn't care, or she felt justified in berating him in public. It apparently had become a habit for her. In response, the man did nothing. He simply stood there and took it, no doubt deeply embarrassed and humiliated.

If you ask most men what they want from their wives, they will say respect. Along with respect comes support. A healthy marriage is about being on the same team and forming a lasting partnership. A woman who blindsides her man finds the trust between them weakened. He feels like he's living with an adversary instead of a helper. Men don't need more pain; the world offers us enough of that. What men need is support. This doesn't necessarily mean a conflict-free relationship, but it does mean working together for a common goal—success of the partnership. My friend, author Bill Perkins, says his wife, Cindy, is a complement to his hard-driving personality. "I am not as hard-edged as I used to be. She [Cindy] brought a tender, gentle side to parenting. I was more the disciplinarian. At times, she understood I needed to take the lead. We didn't argue about how to cope. She was just a good listener."

Another friend, Robert, had almost no support from his wife, Jackie. "If I would tell the kids one thing, Jackie would tell them something else. I tried to talk to her about it, but she just gave me a blank stare. I never felt she respected or supported my efforts with our children. I always thought parenting was a partnership." When a woman refuses to support her husband's efforts in raising children, she sends the message to him and to their children that he's incompetent, ignorant, or unnecessary. He gets the message—and so do the children. This is just another form of rejection. If he tries to take responsibility to be a godly leader in his home, he might be blamed for creating tension or for being overcontrolling. If he gives in to his wife's sense of knowing what's best, the children will suffer. In the end, Robert gave up. The tug-of-war with his wife was too much. As one of his friends told him, "Jackie sabotaged the making of men in your family by refusing partnership and using her paradigm of child-raising preferences to dominate the situation and undermine your attempts at fulfilling your role as the father/male and model/mentor."

5. *A man needs conflicts resolved.* How many times have you seen a couple engage in some seemingly meaningless squabble? I have seen it in older couples, people who have failed to resolve conflicts from long ago. They react to the most trivial of matters. Sure, the reaction is a long-standing habit, but it goes deeper than that. At some point during their marriage, an issue or hurt was stuffed. That's just another way of saying it was pushed under the proverbial carpet of their emotional lives. Men are not omniscient. While a woman may believe a man ought to know what's bothering her, most don't.

We have heard the stereotypes about how men process conflict by fleeing to their shop, a sporting event, or a bar. The truth is that men want to resolve conflicts with their mate, but oftentimes they don't know where to begin. In some instances, they try, and it just gets worse. I stood outside a Home Depot store one day, listening and watching as a woman yelled at her husband. I waited, wondering if he might hit her. He was a big man, standing next to the open door of their truck. The wife got within inches of his face, her voice carrying through the parking lot with anger and disdain. I can't tell you what the argument was about, but I can tell you what I saw. When the conflict reached fever pitch, the husband walked about twenty feet away and then turned around and came back for more. He was, in the words of marriage expert John Gottman, *flooded.* This man's wife was pushing all his emotional buttons, and he wisely walked away for a breather. I was impressed. He never touched her. He just sucked it up as she unloaded both barrels.

Some people are conflict avoiders, determined to keep the peace at any price. They deal with conflict by fleeing. Others seem to thrive on conflict. That's what they saw growing up, so that's what seems normal. They thrive on the rush of adrenaline as their blood pressure skyrockets. Matthew, in his fifties, married a conflict avoider. In his first year of marriage, Sandra ran and hid whenever a disagreement arose. For Matthew, this was baffling behavior. He wanted to find a way to resolve their differences. Since Sandra's family never argued, any form of disagreement seemed like conflict to her. Most men are not content with unresolved conflict. They're wired to try to fix whatever is broken. They may not always do it the right way (whatever that is), but they want to try. This desire for resolution is a positive start for dealing with heart-level issues.

6. *A man needs to feel he's a priority*. This is not some self-centered, egotistical need. It doesn't mean men need attention and service twenty-four hours a day. A man just wants to feel he matters. He wants to know that he's valuable, cherished, and important to his wife—beyond providing a paycheck or helping with household chores. Once a couple has children, the wife often redirects her emotional priorities to their children. It's easy to see how this balancing act between husband and children can get out of balance. It does in many relationships, and the husband ends up feeling unnecessary and unappreciated. Often, his needs go unmet. Rarely is this a conscious decision on the part of the wife, but the effect is no less hurtful.

A wife must keep in mind that her marital relationship should be her number one priority. As the husband and wife make the marriage relationship a priority, the family unit will grow proportionately in strength. Strength begets strength. Conversely, if a man feels like an outsider, tension and conflict will grow. It produces dysfunction and insecurity where there should be strength and vitality.

Mel never felt like a priority in his house. Lynn was always too busy for him, and he knew it. On the rare occasions when they had sex, it was after 10 p.m., and Lynn was exhausted. Mel felt he was always getting the leftovers. He felt cheated. The relationship began to go downhill until both ended up in counseling. Lynn felt justified about putting all her energy into the household, her work, or the children. She equated her hard work and effort as building the partnership, but instead her efforts resulted in unraveling the relationship. An overcommitted woman is one who soon finds love and passion gone.

7. *A man needs companionship.* The best marriages are those that begin with a solid friendship. The idea of friendship presupposes common interests and a willingness to grow together. A man does not look to a woman to fill his needs for a male friend; he looks to the woman to fulfill his needs for intimate companionship. He wants to share his life. In turn, he wants her to share her life with him. This doesn't mean either relinquishes separate interests. Ideally, common interests draw them together and keep them together, but this takes a conscious decision and follow-through.

My friends, Dr. John and Ginny Moody, have a mutually satisfying relationship because they invest in one another. They enjoy kayaking, learning, travel, concerts, and hiking together. They also enjoy separate interests, John with his garden and Ginny with her music. Other married couples, whose relationships thrive, manage to find places to connect. Those relationships that don't grow end up with couples living parallel lives—each doing what he wants or she wants. They soon become little more than roommates. This is clearly not God's idea of a happy or healthy marriage, and it's not want men want or need.

8. *A man needs respect.* In order of priority, the need for respect is near the top of the list. Dr. Emerson Eggerichs says

women want unconditional love, but men need unconditional respect. He explains that a woman wants a man to be sensitive and caring but often goes about getting her needs met in a counterproductive way. "Unfortunately a wife's usual approach is to complain and criticize in order to motivate her husband to become more loving," writes Eggerichs.[2] A wife cannot motivate through criticism. And a husband is not encouraged by ridicule, shame, or manipulation. A man responds the same way any other human being does—through kindness, patience, and encouragement.

There are many ways a woman can show disrespect. She may undermine her husband with the children, humiliate him in public, or nag him until he emotionally withdraws. For a man, respect takes on many forms. It includes encouragement, support, physical intimacy, kindness, and making him feel like he's a priority. It means focusing on the big picture rather than nitpicking the small, bothersome things. Again, Eggerichs writes, "When a wife doesn't speak 'respect language,' after awhile her husband isn't interested in communicating. Who wants to keep talking to someone who doesn't speak your language?" He concluded, "It's high time for women to start discovering how their husbands really feel."[3]

Feeling Let Down

"Praise of men is an endangered species. But the good about men is not. And when something good is being endangered it needs special attention,"[4] wrote Warren Farrell in his book, *Why Men Are the Way They Are*. If a man does not feel respect or appreciation, he will find it any way he can—often in the company of other men.

In the dark movie *Fight Club*, the character played by Brad Pitt gives a brief lecture to a basement full of men waiting to fight—for the fun of it. These men of varying ethnic backgrounds have come to test themselves as men. They want and need to feel alive. They're numb from the mundane routines of life, weary of feeling marginal. They feel displaced, disappointed, but most of all disappointed in themselves. Pitt launches into his speech by saying, "I see all this potential squandered . . . an entire generation pumping gas, waiting tables, slaves with white collars . . . we're the middle children of history man, no purpose or place. We have no great war, no great depression. Our great war a spiritual war, our great depression our lives. We've been raised on television to believe that one day we'd all be millionaires and movie gods and rock stars. But we won't. We're slowly learning that fact. We're very, very pissed off." So let the games begin.

Most men, if they're honest, will tell you they don't feel they can measure up to the expectations placed upon them—by fathers, by wives, by employers, by children. They go through the motions wondering if someday they will be found out. This is a lousy way to go through life. Most women find this hard to understand. They see men as strong and don't imagine the vulnerability that lies beneath. This is not to say men are trembling wimps inside. To the contrary, most go about their daily duties and perform them well, even dying for causes greater than themselves when duty bids them to do so.

The disillusionment that plagues some men or stifles others often represents false shame and guilt. For others, like the men in *Fight Club*, it's an overarching need to feel something, anything. If a man can't feel good, he will settle for feeling bad, as long as he feels *something*. In another movie, *The Edge*, billionaire Anthony Hopkins finds himself lost in the Alaskan wilderness, hunted by man-eating bears. It's a world away from his plush New York City office. His accidental adventure upends his life, but in a good way. He turns to his cynical companion and says, "What should we do, lie down and die? It puts things in perspective being out here, doesn't it?" Indeed, crisis or adventure forces a man to *feel*—something men are desperate to attain.

At the end of the movie, Hopkins says, "All my life I've wanted to do something unequivocal. I'll tell you what I'm going to do. I'm going to start my life over." Unequivocal! That's what men in today's culture desperately need, though many just don't know it or they have given up on the possibility. Our heavenly Father did something unequivocal, and many didn't recognize it. Oftentimes the unequivocal is surreal. It was for the Pharisees. They had their minds made up about who God was and how he was going to present himself. They wanted the predictable, not the unequivocal. Meanwhile, our culture strives for the predictable but longs for the unequivocal. If the truth be known, men want both; they *need* both.

If all great men face their tests in life, then what happens after they *pass* the test? Ideally, they become more empathetic and mature, less full of themselves and more full of their Creator. They recognize their weakness or insecurity and don't try to hide it. Look at Joseph, Moses, David, Peter, or Paul. They each faced a test and came through in the end. You will too. Our tendency is to act when we should be patient. This was King Saul's mistake—and it cost him the crown, as well as God's presence (see 1 Sam. 15). We want to speed things up, to get out of the unknown and into places we can control. This is precisely why God puts us in situations we cannot control. What was it Christ said to Paul? "My grace is sufficient for you, for my power is made perfect in *weakness*" (2 Cor. 12:9, emphasis added). Notice Christ didn't say, "My power is made perfect in *your* weakness." He simply used the word *weakness*. This is about men understanding their dependency upon the one source of strength that can help them in their time of greatest need, for we find our source of strength in God when we place our trust in him.

Women come to men, but it's not to hear about their weaknesses. They come to absorb their strength. They come for protection. Is it any wonder then that women don't want weak men? The great paradox is that men *are* weak, but it's in their weakness that they must rise up and act strong. Men know this, and most men can do it. Now this is not to say a compassionate woman cannot be what God intends—a helpmeet (or "suitable helper") during times of masculine struggle. But a man must be careful not to invest himself in the wrong place when what he needs most is God.

In our quest to get our personal needs met in a rights-dominated culture, men and women of faith must take their cues from Christ, who willingly gave his own life that others might have life.

Relationships
Minefields of Change

LET ME tell you about Barbara and Oliver Rose . . ."

In *The War of the Roses*, actor Danny Devito plays a divorce attorney. The man he's talking to sits in an expensive leather chair, listening in rapt silence. He could be any man.

"I won't start the clock," Devito tells the man. "My fees are $450 an hour. When a man who makes $450 an hour wants to tell you something for free, you should listen."

The story begins like any other love story, with hope for the future. Yet slowly, almost imperceptibly, it starts to sour. Oliver Rose, played by Michael Douglas, is a colleague of Devito's. Kathleen Turner plays Douglas's wife, Barbara. Oliver is trying to make partner at the law firm where he's employed, so the Roses invite the senior partners for dinner. The hosts are eager to impress. It's during the dinner that Oliver interrupts his wife as she blabbers on nervously about their china. It's a seemingly innocuous event, but she silently fumes. That night, as the two get ready for bed, Oliver says, "Gosh, I hope they didn't notice what a jerk I am." His wife replies, "They never seemed to." It's a telling moment. He takes her comment as a compliment, when it's really a sarcastic snip. Oliver is clueless, and it gets worse.

At some point in their marriage, Barbara decides she's had enough. There is no single cause. Instead, there are many small and unresolved irritants. These escalate into a full-fledged war. The conversation between husband and wife shows how twisted relationships can become.

"I want a divorce," says Barbara.

"Why?"

"I can't give you specific reasons."

"Well, try," says Oliver.

"I don't want to try."

"Did I do something? Did I not do something? Is there somebody else, another man?"

"No."

"I think you owe me a reason. You owe me a solid reason, a reason that makes sense."

"Because when I see you asleep, when I look at you lately, I just want to smash your face in!"

Oliver stares at her as if he's just been run over by a Mack truck. The cynicism, pent-up anger, confusion, the inability to pinpoint specific causes, and the unanswered questions are familiar to many couples.

Recent research suggests Christian marriages are in at least as bad a shape as the relationships of nonchurched people. Christians don't like to admit weaknesses, yet people of faith do have power struggles. They can be selfish, resentful, and fall into despair like anyone else. In this chapter, we will explore the changing nature of relationships. We will look at how recent trends affect marriage in general, and more specifically, at what's happening in Christian marriages. Finally, we will explore ten core qualities that lead to successful marriages.

Relationships in the War Zone

When researcher George Barna first came out with his study about Christians and divorce, many people were upset. In shock and awe, people missed the larger question—what are the reasons that lay behind the data? The most controversial finding in the study is this: "Born-again Christians are more likely to go through a marital split than are non-Christians."[1] The study found divorce less prevalent in the Northeast (19 percent), primarily a Catholic region, than in the South (27 percent) which is the conservative Bible belt. Barna's study found atheists divorce less (21 percent) than Bible-believing Protestants (25 percent).

For all the talk about faithfulness, commitment, and vows, Christians seem oddly insincere in their behaviors. They know divorce hurts kids, but they hear it's better to stay together for the sake of children. Statistics support both of these claims. But if marriage is so important, why are so many not making it? Like any social trend, the reasons are multicausal. This means there is no single answer, and several explanations may be at work to create the result. Christians verbally hold marriage as a sacred covenant, and rightfully so, yet leave little room for dealing with the issues that sabotage a marriage. In other words, they may look good on the outside while struggling with major problems behind closed doors. The myth of perfection, as well as legalism and pride, keep many Christian couples from seeking the help they need. When churches take a stand against divorce, they often forget to take an equally strong stand *for* helping struggling couples. When Christian couples struggle, separate, or divorce, church people don't know how to relate to them. They're caught in a double bind, where nothing they do will be construed as right. If they show mercy, they seem soft on divorce. If they ignore these hurting people, they look uncaring and insensitive. If they judge them, they appear Pharisaical.

Barna explained the pattern of Christians and divorce this way: "Even more disturbing is that when those individuals experience a divorce many of them feel their community of faith provides rejection rather than support." His conclusion: ". . . the high incidence of divorce within the Christian community challenges the idea that churches provide truly practical and life-changing support for marriages."[2] Donald Hughes, the author of *The Divorce Reality*, wrote, "In the churches, people have a superstitious view that Christianity will keep them from divorce, but they're subject to the same problems as everyone else, and they include a lack of relationship skills . . . just being born again is not a rabbit's foot."[3]

A Changing Relational Landscape

At no time in recorded history have marriage relationships been more at risk. Distrust is high, and commitment is low. Selfishness is the rule rather than the exception. Men use women, if not physically, then at least emotionally. Because they remain objects of a man's desire, women often feel used or taken for granted. The result is distrust, anger, disillusionment, self-protection, insecurity, and vying for control. These elements do not form solid relationships. Meanwhile, many Christian relationships, even those that have lasted decades, are stuck in neutral, which is a great place to be if you don't want to get anywhere. And it seems to work for a while, but nothing good ever happens in neutral. For relationships, it's a risky place to be. Eventually, someone has to make a change—to put the relationship in drive. Instead of putting relationships in drive, Christian couples may do just the opposite and go in reverse, and they don't see well when they're headed backwards. The risk of hitting something is greater, and yet, instead of taking their foot off the accelerator, they keep it there, hoping something good will happen. This crazy-making cycle is sometimes too much—for men and women.

In a single week, I spoke with five Christian men who have been married for twenty years or more. In all but one case, they were going through a divorce. Paradoxically, there isn't a single instance of infidelity or financial strain among the group. Carl is a prime example. He's desperately frustrated. At fifty, he's a successful businessman and a genuinely nice guy. He and his wife have gone to counseling in an attempt to shore up their difficulties, but nothing has changed. Carl is dreadfully unhappy with the status quo. He's tired, confused, and looking for answers. Men like Carl want more from their relationships than they're experiencing, and they secretly fear they will never find joy in their present situation. Of course, people can and do change, but usually a crisis is the catalyst. Sometimes it's a personal epiphany or reevaluation of life. Even so, men very rarely create a better relational environment for themselves by giving up quickly. If God can create new life in a man and woman, he can certainly resurrect a dead relationship. The caveat to this change, however, is an equally passionate willingness by both husband and wife to reinvent their relationship. It takes more than commitment to the institution of marriage. It requires a commitment to personal change, but an unwillingness to change is one area where long-lasting Christian relationships are coming unglued.

The men I spoke with are not self-centered egoists looking for greener grass. They're not having a midlife crisis; they're past midlife. They're simply tired of living in relationships that don't satisfy, where their spouse couldn't care less about their wants or needs. If God created men and women to meet one another's need for intimacy, these men feel cheated. I'm sure countless Christian women feel the same. I know, without a doubt, that men can be selfish and inattentive to the needs of their wives. But the trend I see is men who are deeply frustrated, and they're reevaluating. In most instances, they're trying hard to keep their marriages and families together. If they have a sensitive wife, one willing to do the introspective work necessary for the marriage to survive, they will stay married. If not, they will leave. They are part of the divorce pattern within the church. These men want more than an antagonistic relationship in their latter years; they don't want to settle for less than what they believe God intended for them. This phenomenon is a consequence of multiple factors that lead to a relationship disengagement.

Here are some of the major themes I hear from men about their relationships:

1. Their spouse refuses to make reasonable changes (passive intransigence).
2. These couples no longer find enjoyment in being with one another (lack of common interests).
3. They feel beaten down or taken for granted (lack of encouragement or respect).
4. Communication ends in arguments, and nothing is ever resolved (continuous tension).
5. Their marriage lacks intimacy (little or no sex or touching).
6. They feel smothered or trapped (mothered by their spouse).
7. They're depressed, unhappy, or both (they see no reasonable solutions).
8. They're willing to work through differences if there is hope (openness to change).

Christian couples can't keep pretending their marriages will thrive, or even survive, if they don't put in the effort to make them work. This should be self-evident. If there's a flaw in Christian thinking, it's this: Christians believe nothing they do or do not do *should* jeopardize their marriages because they're under a legal or spiritual contract. Certainly, there is truth to this, but they often miss the reciprocal nature of the contract. A man is obliged to remain faithful and committed, but his wife often feels under no obligation to be intimate, respectful, or honoring of her husband. This is but one unspoken assumption in a

Christian relationship, and there are many other wrong assumptions. Call it a false-relationship worldview if you like, but whatever it is, it's like piling wet snow on a steep mountain slope. Eventually, the snow will become so heavy it will give way, tumble down the mountain, and wreak havoc along the way. A Christian can pretend the climatic risks for the avalanche don't exist, but that won't stop it from happening. A better solution is to minimize the risks by clearing the slopes and blasting away at the vulnerable spot with a mortar. It takes an awareness of specific relationship risks and then acting on the awareness to bring change. And men want change! They want to blast away at the accumulating snow so the emotional slopes of their lives will be safe. When a husband feels an avalanche can unload on him at any moment, he prefers not to be in the path of its fury. But a husband can also be his own worst enemy, sowing seeds of anger and mistrust that are not lost on the wife who is unhappily in his path.

Individualism, Freedom, Responsibility, and Personal Rights

A fifty-two-year-old Christian professional that I'll call Bud is a good example of why relationships can seem like minefields. Men and women are confused. A female friend sent me a copy of Bud's comments about his wife: "I thought I could help you by being your friend, but now I realize you're like an alcoholic or drug addict. Until you see your own problem as being your problem and nobody else's and want to change and go get professional help, you'll never enjoy the thrill and passion of a good, healthy relationship." Bud went on to say, "You haven't been a friend, and therefore I'm not losing a thing. Unless you consider losing a miserable, self-centered, complaining person out of my life a loss. I consider it an MLK moment: 'Free at last! Free at last!' "

My first reaction to reading the full text was one of shock. Do men really talk like this to women? Yes, men do, and it doesn't foster closer bonds or trust between husband and wife. Bud's comments are insensitive, defensive, mean-spirited, and anything but Christlike. I can see how some women become cynical and wonder whether there are any good men out there. Yes, there are psychos who pose as Christians. There are predators in nightclubs, but they're also in our churches. These angry men think they know how to treat women. Instead, they drive women into an emotional underground. Bud is one of them. He's sick but doesn't know it.

Today's culture is seriously confused about relationships, partly because it doesn't understand the true meaning of personal rights, responsibility, or freedom. Freedom is not the license to do as one pleases. Freedom—divorced from responsibility—is just another form of bondage. This worldview affects the way men and women see their relationships. If they live according to a postmodern worldview, their relationship is hard pressed to survive. These men and women think they have the right (based on our unlimited personal freedom) to do whatever they please, whatever feels good. This is a transitory definition of happiness, and it keeps some men and women continually looking for the elusive perfect mate.

Individualism, with its subjective definitions, offers little stability. As alternative relationships supplant traditional models of marriage, the original becomes less binding. Eric is a good example. He's twenty-seven years old and does not intend to marry anytime soon. When I asked him why, he said, "Why should I?" He sees no benefit in repeating the mistakes of his parents or countless others who bought into no-fault divorce. He doesn't believe in war, in marriage, in politics, or in traditionalism. He claims to believe in environmental causes, social programs, and freedom. The relationship legacy of the 1970s—abortion-on-demand ("my body, my choice"), no-fault divorce, and women's rights ("a woman needs a man like a fish needs a bicycle")—left newer generations to figure out relationships on their own terms. They have bagged traditionalism because they have seen it fail. Now they're finding that "hooking up" (sex without commitment) and "hanging out" (residence without marriage) doesn't work long-term. They ache for the same thing you and I ache for—intimacy in our relationships—because our Creator made us this way.

The children who survived millions of abortions since 1973 may suffer from a collective "survivor's guilt" or sense that they should matter, or that they should be doing something profound to justify their existence. And they do matter, according to God, but they seem unconvinced that there's a future and a hope. Their relationships reflect this despair, and as a result, rampant individualistic mind-sets prevail.

When I asked Eric, "What do you believe in?" he admitted, "I don't know." For him, nothing is transcendent, nothing is sacred, nothing is fixed, nothing is absolute. Acceptance and tolerance for anyone's idea of truth is what many in this generation believe. For them, relationships are about filling a painful emotional void, even if temporarily. Yet the void is ultimately spiritual, and only spiritual wholeness can salve the wounds of a hurting generation.

This leaves us with a question that begs asking: If relationships are minefields, what are the minesweepers? What does it take to make relationships work in our postmodern era?

What Makes Marriages Work?

How does one quantify a concept like love? In his letter to the Corinthians, the apostle Paul summed it up like this: "Love is patient, love is kind. It does not envy, it does not boast, it is not proud. It is not rude, it is not self-seeking, it is not easily angered, it keeps no record of wrongs. Love does not delight in evil but rejoices with the truth. It always protects, always trusts, always hopes, always perseveres" (1 Cor. 13:4–7).

Why do some couples seem to float effortlessly through their relationships, while others move from one crisis to the next? What are the ingredients of successful marriages? Let's look at the qualities that make successful marriages and that create healthy, enduring relationships.

1. Good conflict-resolution skills
2. Successful communication
3. Mutually shared interests and personal growth
4. Trust
5. Physical affirmation
6. Respect and encouragement
7. Nurturing
8. Selflessness
9. Latitude to pursue individual interests
10. Common goals and plans, accompanied by a commitment to success

A relationship is a living organism. God wants this organism to thrive and grow. Yet social pressures militate against the organism's success. As today's culture redefines marriage as something other than one man and one woman in a legally committed relationship, it weakens the organism by leaving offspring confused. Traditional marriage offers stability to children, safety and protection to women, and generally leads to more responsible behavior in men.

1. Good Conflict-Resolution Skills

Men want to fix things, people, and relationships. They're wired to tinker, to fix, to figure out. Women are wired to feel, to understand. A typical conflict scenario looks something like this: A man comes home from work, and his wife says, "I had a horrible day today. It felt like my boss was out to get me. The kids are driving me nuts, and I am so upset we can't afford to take the vacation to Hawaii like we planned." The wife is simply unloading. Her train-of-consciousness sentences are too much for him to process. He wants data—just the facts. So he's thinking, "What does she mean that her boss was out to get her? What did he do? What did she do? Did he make a pass at her?" There are a million possibilities, and he doesn't have sufficient information to help her fix the problem. What he doesn't understand is that she doesn't want him to fix the problem. She just wants him to listen. She wants to blow off some steam and get her husband to empathize with how she feels.

The same general rules apply regarding her comments about the kids. He will wonder, "What did they do—launch a baseball through the window, plug the toilet, get in a fight at school?" If he doesn't have enough information, his mind goes through countless scenarios. If she doesn't provide detail, he will draw false conclusions, both factually and emotionally. And then his mind jumps to the failed Hawaiian trip. "What does she mean about the vacation in Hawaii? What is she trying to tell me?" Then he comes to the conclusion, "She thinks I'm a loser because we can't afford a nice vacation." Now he's the one who's feeling bad. And so he does what any man would do: He becomes defensive. He believes she's attacking his ability to provide for his family, so he asks, "What did you do to make your boss mad at you?" Then he adds, "Why don't you stop harping on me about the kids and just deal with it?"

All she wanted was to share her feelings, and now he's all bent out of shape. Instead of helping her carry an emotional load, he's attacked her. In a voice that's raised a few decibels, she asks, "What's *your* problem?" Then she leaves the room and determines that her man is no place to trust her feelings. She withdraws. The conflict blows out of proportion because neither spouse sought to understand the other. The element of empathy was missing.

In a conflict-avoidant family, few serious issues are ever resolved. Conflict, disagreements, hurts—they all simmer just below the surface like a big toxic stew. A confrontational family argues about everything. When a conflict-avoidant woman marries a confrontational man, the wife shuts down, retreats, runs away, and always seems to feel hurt. She becomes the perfect victim. She feels overwhelmed and flooded. Healthy marriages learn how to manage conflict and disagreement, while maintaining respect for one another. A conflict-avoidant wife thinks she is setting boundaries by refusing to engage in discussion. The husband interprets this as rejection. He sees it as her unwillingness to take the relationship seriously. All relationships have conflict. In those relationships where conflict is not present, either one or both spouses are probably not having their needs met. Someone is capitulating to the stronger personality, and this is rarely positive. It signals that one partner has given up what's personally important in an effort to maintain peace.

2. Successful Communication

How can a couple resolve conflict when they can't communicate successfully? Women tend to be the communicators, while men tend to keep their feelings to themselves. Girls excel at verbal communication, even in elementary years. They practice it—on anyone who will listen, or even appears to listen. If relationships are going to work, husbands need to learn to listen, and *not to fix* their wives. They must empathize with feelings instead of trying to reinterpret them, as men so often do. Yet, men want to be heard every bit as much as women. Women often don't realize that men have intense emotions, and I don't just mean anger. The emotions of men are no less valid than women's.

When couples seek to communicate on a heart level, even when they disagree, they feel their spouse has heard them. Husbands have to be more forthcoming about opening the secret places of their heart—their dreams, fears, or vulnerabilities. Wives, on the other hand, must be willing to accept this openness in a nonjudgmental way.

3. Mutually Shared Interests

John and Ginny go to concerts and plays together, and they both enjoy hiking, kayaking, and reading. They have maintained a healthy lifestyle into their fifties, so they can continue to do the things that bring them joy as a couple. Another couple I know live parallel lives, meaning they each have their own separate interests, which they pursue to the exclusion of any mutual interests or activities. They're more like roommates than husband and wife. They do have some mutual friends, but they rarely get together with them to do anything. Not surprisingly, the husband, also in his fifties, confided in me that if his wife ever died, he already knew a woman who would be perfect for him. He even talks with her every week. If this sounds like a strange way to manage a marriage after thirty years, you're right. He's living on the edge by having, in effect, an imaginary affair.

Mutual interests are often the glue that hold a good marriage together. Shared experiences accumulate over the years and form a bond that withstands the inevitable pressures of life. Mike, now in his forties, told me his wife rarely does anything with him. He said, "When we first got married, we used to do all kinds of activities together, like hiking and camping. Today, she refuses to do anything except sit in front of the TV." One way couples grow together is to learn new activities or to cross over into activities their mate enjoys. This doesn't mean a woman has to memorize the names of all the World Series winners since 1952, nor does it mean a man has to learn how to ballroom dance. It does mean that both must step outside their comfort zone to enter the other's world.

Allen, another friend of mine, just turned sixty. He recently bought a Harley and asked his wife, Sharlene, if she would learn to ride if he purchased a second bike. When she agreed, he was excited. Now the two of them take trips together, finding pleasure in a shared interest.

4. Trust

As children, individuals start out being trustful, for God made us to be trusting. As they grow up, things happen, and they learn *not* to trust. When they carry that distrust into marriage, the relationship is doomed from the outset. If they aren't confident that their spouse will not cheat or lie, how can they have a vibrant relationship? Some people come into a marriage already damaged from past trust issues. When they bring this baggage into a marriage, it works like a cancer. It took Jeremy twenty years to figure out that his wife, Marilyn, never seemed to trust him. She called his office to check on him, asked whom he talked to when he went to the store, and riffled through his mail. Jeremy put up with Marilyn's behavior for years, not understanding she had misplaced trust issues based on her own insecurity. And Marilyn didn't understand that either. Instead of getting help for her lack of trust, she allowed it to eat her up inside. Clearly, some husbands destroy trust by making unwise choices, and once trust is compromised, it requires conscious effort, counseling, and time to restore it. But a marriage where trust is absent, whether deservedly or not, is one that will either crumble completely or at least fail to achieve optimal vitality.

When a woman communicates mistrust to her husband, he begins to feel like a child. Men don't want to be treated like children. They don't want the smothering, mothering, domineering hand of their wives creeping into the corners of their lives. This degrades men and makes them feel like fleeing. It certainly doesn't create a bond of closeness.

5. Physical Affirmation

A *Newsweek* cover story discussed the increasing number of married women who are choosing to be unfaithful to their husbands. "The road to infidelity is paved with unmet expectations about sex, love and marriage," say the authors.[4] Unmet expectations? Everyone has them. As I said earlier, expectations aren't necessarily bad; in fact, they're part of any relationship. The bigger question is whether a wife can learn to adjust her expectations to make the relationships work. Men have expectations for physical intimacy, and if a relationship is going to work, this need must be met.

Janet, a forty-six-year-old Christian wife and mother, refused to have sex with her husband, Jake. Her reason? She didn't feel unconditional love from him. When I met Jake, he was about ready to explode. They were both involved in full-time ministry, but Jake feared his marriage and ministry life were over. That's how bad it had become. I'm sure in Janet's mind she had very good reasons for turning him away. Yet what she was doing was deconstructing their marriage. This kind of refusal by Christian women is wrong; dare I use the word *sinful*? It's far more common than many people think. Janet sowed the seeds of resentment and anger. She created the emotional climate for Jake to have an affair (though, he didn't). Fortunately, they went to counseling and worked through their problems. What is my point? Christian women must assume responsibility for meeting the physical needs of their husbands.

In marriages that thrive, spouses recognize each other's sexual needs and respond to them—whether they feel like it or not. I'm not saying a woman has to engage in sexual activities with which she is not comfortable. Rather love necessitates that a

man and woman respond to one another's needs for sexual intimacy. Dr. Emerson Eggerichs wrote, "As a wife, you spell respect
to your husband when you appreciate his sexual desire for
you."[5] A woman will say she cannot respond to her husband if
he doesn't meet her emotional needs. This is nonsense. When are
a woman's emotional needs not met? Is there some way to quantify these needs? A man doesn't know. A woman can use the
"emotional needs" angle the same way she does a headache to
avoid physical intimacy. It's too vague. This is not to say a wife
who suffers genuine abuse from her husband is going to feel like
meeting his sexual needs. She won't, and most men understand
this, or ought to.

6. Respect and Encouragement

The men I know aren't sniveling wimps who need steady attention and emotional reinforcement. They do need to know their
contribution to the marriage or to the family is meaningful. How
hard is it for a wife to say, "Honey, I'm glad to have you in my
life," "You're a terrific father," or "I am proud of you"? Why is
it so difficult to express what they feel? Affirmation never diminishes the affirmer. And affirmation is not something men discern
or connect to by emotional osmosis. They cannot go through life
assuming their spouse, children, or friends "just know" how
they feel. Speak it out. A husband needs to know that his wife
supports him, both inside and outside the home.

Tom is fifty-one, and his marriage began to unravel when his
wife pitted the children against him. This is not respect; this is
undermining the very foundation of a relationship. A home
should never be a war of us-against-them. Today Tom says, "A
wife should honor her husband in front of the children even
when he isn't around. She would talk behind my back and put
me down. She planted the seeds, which caused doubt in the children. Both of us have a role designed by God for the family. But

the moment we started trying to fulfill the other person's role, it caused problems."

The dilemma in Tom's home reminds him of his own home as a child. "I remember being so resentful of my mom for bad-mouthing my dad. I grew up resenting that. My son now sees he must put everything Mom says through a filter. He realizes Dad had his faults, but Mom had hers too. Unfortunately, it caused a lot of unnecessary pain. We have lost roles in the family. If you do it the way God designed, nobody is underneath anyone's feet. There is a correct way to build a house. But if you mess with this foundation, the house will eventually fall."

7. Nurturing

Nurturing means a couple invests in each other's emotional and spiritual health. It means they promote the development of the relationship. They feed goodness into one another. It's the care and feeding of each other's soul. It's listening. It's sacrificing. It's recognizing a spouse's needs and validating them. When a couple nurtures one another, they invest in emotional capital. They make deposits into the life of the person they love. When a couple chooses to do so, they strengthen the relationship. Of course, the opposite can also be true. A relationship is like a bank account. A couple can't keep taking money out if they don't make deposits. Too many married folks want only the dividends and neglect to make the deposits. Relationships endure when couples refuse to take each other for granted. They grow stronger when they refuse to make excuses for not investing in one another.

8. Selflessness

Self-centeredness is a relationship destroyer. It's part of humanity's fallen human nature to want things in their own selfish way. Successful relationships require sacrifice, a word rarely heard anymore. How can a relationship work between two selfish people? A couple must be committed to making it work. They must be committed beyond mere words. They must be willing to do the hard work, and that requires working together for the common good. It is, as I said earlier, a quid pro quo kind of relationship. Both husband and wife simultaneously give and receive greater benefits from subjugating their will to the greater good. It works because it's the way God intends it to work.

In his book, *Men Are from Mars, Women Are from Venus*, Dr. John Gray writes, "Given the opportunity to prove his potential he [a man] expresses his best self. Only when he feels he cannot succeed does he regress back to his old selfish ways. When a man is in love, he begins to care about another as much as himself. He's suddenly released from the binding chain of being motivated for himself alone and becomes free to give to another, not for personal gain, but out of caring. He experiences his partner's fulfillment as if it were his own."[6] Gray is right. Men can be selfless if they feel loved. A man will give almost anything for the woman he loves. If he doesn't feel loved or appreciated, he eventually gives up his self-sacrificial ways. Though some men fall into the extreme saints or masochists category, the majority do not. Most react much like other men would react in similar situations, responding with selflessness when they're loved and appreciated by the woman in their life.

9. Pursue Separate Interests

Solid marriages require both mutually shared interests and separate interests. Individual expression and outside interests are good for a relationship. Couples who give their spouse room to explore and grow find their mate is more content and therefore more receptive to their needs. Jeff and Sharon are good examples of balance in relationship. Jeff enjoys mountain biking, court sports, and kayaking. Sharon likes golf and scrapbooking.

Together, they garden, ride bikes, and share responsibilities in the kitchen.

It's okay for husbands and wives to use some of their free time to pursue their own interests. A man doesn't marry to find a clone, nor does he expect his wife to engage in all his activities or interests. A man shouldn't feel guilty for golfing with his friends or watching a game with the guys. And a woman shouldn't feel selfish for going shopping with her friends, taking writing classes, or pursuing other interests. Of course, there is balance to everything. A man who spends every free hour in front of the TV watching ESPN is not just pursuing his own separate interest, he's being selfish, and a selfish man is unattractive.

10. Common Goals and Plans

According to John Gottman, it's how people interact that helps predict the eventual success or failure of a relationship. "Couples need to feel they're building something together that has meaning. How does a relationship support what you see as a mission in life?"[7] While common goals include your children, they must be bigger than that. Eventually children move out, or hopefully they do! A parent (usually the wife) who lives exclusively for the children is asking for trouble. Children should not be the only component of joy or connectedness in a relationship. A marriage where children are the center of the universe is a marriage headed for trouble. I'm not saying a woman (or a man, for that matter) shouldn't make their children a priority. I'm saying children should not supplant the primary relationship between husband and wife.

Common goals should be big and small. Future planning gives couples something to work toward and look forward to *together*. A man shouldn't underestimate the importance of shared plans with his mate. These plans include children while they're at home, but long-range plans are also important. Once children leave, couples who have a long-range plan find greater levels of satisfaction in their relationship. If a wife ignores her husband's needs while their children are younger, he can become resentful. While some men develop a misplaced jealousy at being displaced by their own children, the majority learn how to adapt. A man does this through finding other interests. While his wife might interpret this as irresponsibility, it's often just a coping mechanism. Couples that share common goals find greater emotional connectedness through shared experience. As spouses share a common history of positive or challenging experiences, they form a tighter bond between them.

Searching for the Perfect One

Most men are romantics. They want the whole package every bit as much as women do. There is just one problem: there is no perfect person. In fact, there is no perfect relationship because there is no completely unselfish person. Nor is there anyone who can perfectly fulfill every need, want, or desire a man has. Beneath the surface of most relationships, there is gunk, like the buildup of carbon on a carburetor. Too much of it begins to affect performance.

In her book, *Trapped in the Magic Mirror,* Deborah Dunn wrote that the gunk often builds up because couples develop unrealistic expectations about relationships. She also said men are just as addicted to romance as women. Dunn encouraged men and women to learn to overcome a romanticized worldview, one the media keeps placing in front of them as if it were the standard to live by. To wives she says, "We become addicted to an endless narcissistic cycle of perfectionism and attention-getting in order to feel worthy and valued, and it's our husbands who bear the burdens of our cravings. Even when we do get attention from our husbands, we're starting to discover it's not enough."[8]

No wonder some husbands turn to pornography or other false thrills. Many believe anything is better than what they have. These men think every husband is having better sex, making more money, and has smarter kids than he does. In most instances, this too is a façade. The good news, or bad news for some, is that these idealistic fantasies are mostly wrong. And the sooner men come to realize this, the sooner they begin to embrace a form of contentment that stabilizes them emotionally. As a husband works to understand his needs, to change himself, to submit to his Creator, and to extend himself in sacrificial love, God works on his behalf. A man's success in marital relationships is God's will, and a man's success becomes his way of honoring God.

Pulling It All Together

R APHAEL IS in his fifties and is old enough to look back at his life and what matters most. He says, "All good things flow from having a clearly defined sense of honor . . . from having a strong sense of personal integrity. You cannot develop emotionally or spiritually without a sense of honor." It isn't the things a man owns or how he looks that ultimately define him. Rather, it's the internal issues of the heart. These are what matter—eternally. Call it honor, integrity, character, or all three, but a man must master these through the hundreds of choices he makes every day.

If he's wise, he asks himself what God expects of him. Otherwise, he so allows the marketplace, other people, or his false perceptions to define him. God spoke clearly to this issue in Micah 6:8: "He has showed you, O man, what is good. And what does the Lord require of you? To act justly and to love mercy and to walk humbly with your God."

There we have it. In two simple lines, we learn what God expects of us. How much more clearly does our Creator have to lay it out for us? Why do we keep fumbling, failing, and becoming frustrated when the path is so clearly marked? My guess is that the answer falls into two categories. First, we expect the answers to be big or complicated. They aren't. They're actually quite simple, but also hard to do. This brings me to the second reason—we find justice, mercy, and humility difficult to do. Mercy means giving people what they don't deserve—a break, love, kindness. These values of honor, character, or whatever you want to call them are tough. Men don't do mercy well. We do vengeance, anger, or payback better. No wonder we prefer *Diehard, Dirty Harry*, and *Lethal Weapon* to movies that explore relationship dynamics. That's just not the way most guys are wired.

To make matters worse, humility is no less easy than mercy. It's not exactly the first word that comes to mind when one thinks about masculinity. For most males, it implies weakness, not strength. Men are supposed to be strong . . . we think. But a man's definition of strength doesn't always coincide with God's definition. And this is why I have such a problem with the way most churches portray Christ—as a weakling. Visualize the pictures that show Jesus knocking at the door, long hair flowing, a kindly look on his face. Today's churches perpetuate this image. If Jesus is such a weakling, men don't want to follow him. Did you ever wonder why it's so tough to get men out for a men's meeting? Men prefer something a bit more activity-oriented. Churches miss the mark when they try to attract men to meetings and countless hours of sitting on their posteriors, listening to someone drone on about what they ought to be doing.

Try to develop another picture in your mind, not just the one of Jesus that you saw in *The Passion of the Christ* (suffering) or the one you see of him knocking at the door. Picture him completely. Picture him knocking over the tables of the money changers, as people scatter and money falls to the ground. Imagine him tearing apart the religious leaders with a verbal licking, his jugular vein bulging, his eyes ablaze with anger. Yes, these are portraits of Christ too. And that's okay. You need not fear these parts of your Savior. You need not erase these segments of the Bible, for they show a more complete picture. I doubt Jesus was smiling when he called the religious leaders blind guides, white-washed tombs, snakes, a brood of vipers, and hypocrites (see Matt. 23). I think you can safely say that he didn't mince words; he told it like it was. And you don't need to defend his actions. You do need, however, to accept that this was part of who he was when he walked this earth.

Contemporary churches tend to focus on God's feminine characteristics, and then wonder why men aren't interested in coming to church. On the one hand, they emphasize love, joy, kindness, patience, gentleness, grace, and mercy—all true attributes of God. But they also need to show the traditional masculine qualities like justice, anger, frustration, forcefulness, and destruction (remember the flood?). These qualities usually are shoved under the rug. Many churches dichotomize God's attributes to fit more neatly into a preconceived notion of what they *want* him to be. By reinforcing this partial view of God, they alienate men.

But can today's church do better? Yes, if they will begin to show that the Bible is God's way of revealing himself—his whole self, not just the so-called palatable parts. And yes, he was meek and mild, but he was also forceful and strong. Men can be forceful and strong without apologizing for it. Many churches inadvertently drive the passion out of men and end up encouraging them to serve a passionless Christ. Churches tell men to turn the other cheek but not to stand passionately against injustice. They somehow see love and anger as mutually exclusive, though that isn't necessarily true. Men are mostly bored in church because churches often don't meet their needs. If you think I'm off base, ask yourself how much of your church's budget goes to programs directed toward men.

After a weekend seminar sponsored by a parachurch group, Jake came to my place to process his experience. It was mostly positive, and he was thrilled with the emotional baggage he managed to unload while at the seminar. I've known Jake for six years and find him to be kind, honorable, willing to learn, and a genuinely good man. When I told him my impression of him, Jake said, "That's just the problem. I'm too nice. I don't stand up for myself when I should." What a revelation! Yet I fear Jake is suffering from the same mental-masculine confusion that comes from trying to understand what it means to be a Christian man. This isn't some twentysomething guy trying to discover himself. Jake is in his early fifties and is only now asking the questions that come after a man has looked deep inside himself. Often, men find the ghosts that have animated their choices and want finally to expose and exorcise them. Some men ultimately do, and they learn that while it's okay to be vulnerable, kind, compassionate, and merciful, it's also okay to be passionate, strong, and driven.

Before Jake left, I told him I would rather have a man like him as a friend than one who is arrogant, greedy, angry, and afraid to confront his demons. The conversation with Jake reminded me of another important part of masculinity, one that rarely, if ever, gets enough emphasis—friendship and sharing. These two attributes are desperately needed by men. I don't mean the kind of friendship where the blind are leading the blind into endless hours of watching sports on television; I mean the kind of heart sharing that occurs when two men become vulnerable with one another. It's when they share their deepest desires, hurts, and fears, which they need to do regularly. A certain bond develops when men are vulnerable with each other. They learn that their world is not all that different from anyone else's. The Promise Keepers movement touched on this, but it wasn't enough. Men don't really care about being a part of a movement. They want to be part of something more personal than that, something where they can recover from a sense of lostness by finding each other. Men without close male friends are disconnected. They cannot find balance because they lack perspective about what it means to be a man. They lose sight of the fact that there are countless other men who feel the same as they do, wondering if they're on the right road and asking themselves if they're okay. Men must tell other men they're okay when they are. Men can and should share their pain. They can encourage one another, mentor younger men and boys, and learn to accept that masculinity is not a pathology for which they must apologize, but it's a God-given gift that they can harness for his purposes.

Along with friendship there is something else that has been a theme throughout this book—encouragement. Men need it, though they often don't get it. What they do get is plenty of negativity from the world. If a man is hammered at work and underappreciated at home, he's not getting his need for appreciation met. He may go into depression or look for an emotional fix elsewhere, but eventually he will break—one way or another. Men can be a lifeline to each other by sharing openly and honestly the good things they see in one another. I realize most men aren't into expressing their feelings, but as I said earlier in the book, men see themselves differently than others see them. I'm not suggesting they pump one another up emotionally like football players before a game; rather, I'm talking about verbal expression of character truth. How else are men to know if they're making the grade? I wish that type of knowledge were intuitive for each man, but it's not.

In working with elementary- and middle school–aged boys, I've discovered a pattern. They often do not believe the good things I point out about them. I don't make these items up to build some false sense of self-esteem. These affirmations take many forms. For example, before one boy got into my car, he knocked the snow off his boots. No big deal, but how many boys would think to do that? I told him I appreciated it and reinforced his thoughtfulness to his mother. Parents often hear the bad stuff their boys are doing, but rarely do they hear someone else bragging on them. Men need to do this more often, with other men as well as with boys. I can't begin to tell you how many times I've heard a young boy say, "I'm a loser" or "I'm stupid." I immediately ask, "Who told you that?" I don't think any boy has ever told me that is what his mom or dad said; rather, it's how they *feel* about themselves. Men can help change this negative pattern by encouraging hope. As men, we can be champions of other men and boys. We can build up our sons, our fathers, our fathers-in-law, or friends. The effort costs us nothing.

My friend Allen is always looking for ways to bless my sons. He has engaged them in conversation or teasingly played with them since they were young. I wanted my sons to feel that other men noticed and cared about them. I'm sure you want the same for your sons. A friend of mine told me he ran into my oldest son, Justin. He mentioned that Justin looked great, his weight loss was a real plus, and that he seemed happy. I asked if he told Justin what he told me. He said he hadn't. All I'm saying here is that men need to verbalize the positive actions or character qualities they see in one another. This encouragement is not difficult. So why don't men do it? Remember, men don't get all their emotional needs met through women. Men get their emotional needs met through other men too, just as women do through other women.

As you navigate your way through life or help your sons with their route finding, remember that the world does not define who you are as a man. Your wife doesn't define you, nor does your mother, your grade-school teachers, or your boss. The only opinion that really matters is what God thinks. As you seek to honor him, the path becomes clearer. This does not mean the path won't be strewn with obstacles along the way. It will. And these obstacles will seem to enter your path at the most inauspicious times. When they do, you need to remind yourself that *predictability is the enemy of genuine adventure.* And you must begin to *see the pitfalls of life as stepping-stones to masculine greatness and godly maturity.*

Notes

Introduction

1. David Popenoe, *Life Without Father* (New York: The Free Press, 1996), 2, 197.

2. Sean Elder, "The Lock Box," *Psychology Today*, March/April 2005, 42.

3. Andrew Hacker, *Mismatch* (New York: Scribner, 2004), 189.

Chapter One

1. Carson Pue, *Mentoring Leaders* (Grand Rapids, MI: Baker Books, 2005), 60.

2. Richard Land, *Imagine! A God-Blessed America* (Nashville, TN: Broadman and Holman, 2005), 86.

Chapter Two

1. Francis Frangipane, *This Day We Fight* (Grand Rapids, MI: Chosen, 2005), 35–37.

2. Robert Bly, *Iron John* (New York: Addison-Wesley, 1990), 17.

3. Ibid., 12, 24.

Chapter Three

1. John Eldredge, *Wild at Heart* (Nashville, TN: Thomas Nelson, 2001), 190.

2. Karina Rollins, "Boys under Attack: Christina Hoff Sommers Was Right," *American Enterprise*, September 2003.

3. Marshall Poe, "The Other Gender Gap," *Atlantic Monthly*, Jan/Feb 2004.

4. "Boys in the Classroom," Michael Thompson, CBS News, quoted from respectyourman.org/education_gap.asp.

5. Ibid.

6. Ibid.

7. Cathy Young, "Where the Boys Are—Concern over Boys in America," *Reason*, February 2001.

8. Jon Scieszka, "Guys Read: Encouraging Boys to Love Books," *All Things Considered*, 12 May 2005.

9. See Rollins.

10. James Dobson, *Bringing Up Boys* (Wheaton, IL: Tyndale House, 2001), 182.

Chapter Four

1. Dan Kindlon, *Raising Cain* (New York: Ballantine, 1999), 6.

2. Don S. Otis, *Teach Your Children Well* (Grand Rapids, MI: Revell, 2000), 3.

3. Brian Molitor, *A Boy's Passage* (Colorado Springs, CO: Shaw, 2001), 33.

4. John Ashcroft, *On My Honor* (Nashville, TN, Thomas Nelson, 1998), 167.

5. Rosey Grier and Kathi Mills, *Winning* (Ventura, CA: Regal Books, 1990), 185.

6. Dobson, *Boys*, 55.

7. Richard Saul Wurman, *Information Anxiety 2* (Indianapolis, IN: Que, 2001), 92.

8. Allan Bloom, *The Closing of the American Mind* (New York: Simon & Schuster, 1987), 86.

9. David French, *A Season for Justice* (Nashville, TN: Broadman and Holman, 2002), 40, 108.

10. Bill Proctor, *The Gospel According to the New York Times* (Nashville, TN: Broadman and Holman, 2000), 23–24.

Chapter Five

1. Andrew Hacker, *Mismatch: The Growing Gulf between Women and Men* (New York: Scribner, 2003), 15.
2. Ibid., 13.
3. David Blankenhorn, *Fatherlessness in America* (New York: Basic Books, 1995), 4.
4. Robert Bly, *Iron John* (Cambridge, MA: De Capo Press, 2004), 146, 151.
5. Rebecca Gardyn, "Almost Adults," *American Demographics*, 1 September 2003.
6. Lance Armstrong, *It's Not about the Bike* (New York: Penguin Putnam, 2000), 18.

Chapter Six

1. Donald McCullough, *Wisdom of the Pelicans* (New York: Viking Compass, 2002), 8.
2. Emerson Eggerichs, *Love and Respect* (Brentwood, TN: Integrity Publishers, 2004), 253.
3. Gail Sheehy, *Understanding Men's Passages* (New York: Random House, 1998), 91.
4. Os Guinness, *The Long Journey Home* (Colorado Springs, CO: WaterBrook, 2001), 67.

Chapter Seven

1. Wurman, *Information Anxiety*, 290.
2. Robert Bork, *Slouching Toward Gomorrah* (New York: Regan Books, 1996), 9.
3. Wurman, *Information*, 15–16.
4. Eldredge, *Wild*, 43.

Chapter Eight

1. Michael Saks, *Social Psychology and Its Applications* (New York: Harper & Row, 1988), 153.
2. Warren Farrell, *The Myth of Male Power* (New York: Simon & Schuster, 1993), 12.
3. See www.respectyourman.org.

4. Anna Quindlen, "The Value of the Outsider," *Newsweek*, 24 October 2005, 86.

5. Lionel Tiger, *The Decline of Males*, 184.

6. Dorothy Kelly Patterson, *The Family* (Nashville, TN: Broadman and Holman, 2002), 71.

7. See respectyourman.org, 7 July 1999.

8. See www.lesliecsarbone.net.

9. Gail Sheehy, *Understanding Men's Passages* (New York: Random House, 1998), 159.

10. Hacker, *Mismatch*, 50.

11. Teri Reisser, *A Solitary Sorrow* (Colorado Springs, CO: Shaw, 1999), 49.

12. Richard Miniter, "Vassar's War Against Women," *The Washington Times*, 22 December 1994.

13. Comments from Life Skills, 27 May 2004, by Bonner County Deputy Prosecutor, Sara Jayne.

14. Daniel Hemel, "Summers Comments on Women and Science Draw Ire," *The Crimson*, 17 January 2005.

15. Connie Schultz, "Can girls achieve their dreams? They must!" *Spokesman-Review*, 22 June 2005.

16. Staci Eldredge, *Captivating: Unveiling the Mystery of a Woman's Soul* (Nashville, TN, Thomas Nelson, 2005), 4.

17. John Leo, "Of men, women, and money," *U.S. News & World Report*, 21 March 2005, 64.

18. Ibid., 64.

19. Wendy Shalit, *A Return to Modesty* (New York: Free Press, 2000), 44.

20. Dobson, *Boys*, 19.

21. Saks, *Social Psychology and Its Applications*, 141.

22. Christina Hoff Sommers, "Victims of Androgyny," *American Enterprise*, June 2000.

23. Kramarae and Treichler, eds. *A Feminist Dictionary* (Kitchner, Ontario: Pandora Press, 1995).

24. www.msmagazine.com, Spring 2005.

Chapter Nine

1. Unnamed, "American singles cold shoulder romance: survey," from Agence France Press, quoted from research by Pew Internet and American Life Project (13 February 2006), http://afp/afplifestylevalentine.

2. Staci Eldredge, *Captivating*, 161.

3. Eggerichs, *Respect*, 253.

4. Farrell, *The Myth of Male Power*, 264.

5. Ibid., 267.

6. Bly, *Iron John*, 156.

7. Frangipane, *This Day We Fight*, 85–86.

8. Dorothy Kelly Patterson, *The Family*, 37–38.

Chapter Ten

1. Farrell, *Male Power*, 19.

2. Caitlin Flanagan, "Boys Will Be Boys," *Atlantic Monthly*, November 2005, 161–62.

3. Ibid.

4. Katie Roiphe, "Is Maureen Dowd Necessary?" (www.slate.com/id/2129290, 2 November 2005.

5. Proctor, *Gospel*, 163.

6. Ibid., 44–45.

7. Meghan Caldwell, "The Male-Bashing Trend: The Negative Portrayal of Primetime Male Television Sitcom Characters," *Ethics Monthly International*, 23 June 2004, modified.

8. Dobson, *Boys,* 179.

9. See www.focusonyourchild.com.

10. Caldwell, *Wisdom of the Politicians*, 7.

11. Bly, *Iron John*, 23.

12. Ross Parke and Armin Brott, *Throwaway Dads* (New York: Houghton Mifflin Company, 1999), 99.

13. Marie Winn, *The Plug-In Drug* (New York: Penguin, 2002), 158.

14. Robert Bellah, *Habits of the Heart* (Berkeley, CA: University of California Press, 1985), 279.

15. Bernard Goldberg, *Bias* (Washington, DC: Regnery, 2001), 133–34, 137.

16. Roselind Barnett and Caryn Rivers, *Same Difference* (New York: Basic Books, 2004), 43–44.

Chapter Eleven

1. Eggerichs, *Respect,* 252.

2. Ibid., 17.

3. Ibid., 66.

4. Farrell, *The Myth of Male Power,* 22.

Chapter Twelve

1. "Christians Are More Likely to Experience Divorce Than Are Non-Christians," 21 December 1999, *The Barna Update,* www.barna.org.

2. www.valleyskeptic.com/christdivorce.html.

3. www.religioustolerance.org/chr_dira.html.

4. Lorraine Ali and Lisa Miller, "The Secret Lives of Wives," *Newsweek,* 12 July 2004, 50.

5. Eggerichs, *Respect,* 251.

6. John Gray, *Men Are from Mars, Women Are from Venus* (New York: HarperCollins, 1992), 45–46.

7. John Gottman, *Psychology Today,* September/October 2005, 53.

8. Deborah Dunn, *Trapped in the Magic Mirror* (Colorado Springs, CO: Cook, 2006), 53.